# THE ANATOMY OF

Ribs

Spine
(Vertebrae)

Kidneys

Small
Intestine

Colon

Hip Bone
(Pelvis)

Bladder

Testes

Penis

Tail Bones
(Coccygeal)

Femur

Liver

Stomach

Kneecap
(Patella)

Hindlimb
(Tibia)

Hindlimb
(Fibula)

Metatarsis

Digits
(Phalanges)

# Maine Coon Cat

◇

*By Tracey K Hayman*

# Contents

PUBLISHED IN THE UNITED KINGDOM BY:

## INTERPET
PUBLISHING

Vincent Lane, Dorking    Surrey RH4 3YX    England

ISBN 1-84286-011-9

Photographs by Isabelle Français, Cheryl Ertelt, Alan Robinson, Erin Winters,
Ursula Spieker, Brigitte Meier, Rosita Tendieck, Monika Priller, Karin Horeth,
and Hedi Schiefer with additional photographs by
The Animal Health Trust of England, M W Brim, Cat Fanciers Association,
Carolina Biological Supply, Fleabusters Rx for Fleas, J R Hayden, RBP, Interpet,
Dwight R Kuhn, Dr Dennis Kunkel, Phototake, Renate Remplein,
Jean Claude Revy and W B Saunders Company.

Special thanks all the owners of the cats in this book, including Mainly Silver
(Mike and Bonnie Pilar), Gingercats (Ginny Erts), vom Donautal, Lochnargar,
Rottaler, von Racoon and vom Blautal Maine Coons.

# History of the

# MAINE COON CAT

At the turn of the 19th century, the Maine Coon was a hardy cat much valued as an efficient exterminator of rodents. The cat fancy as we know it had yet to begin, and Maine was still awaiting American statehood. The majority of these cats were working mousers and pets in coastal ports, villages and the nearby surrounding farming communities.

For cats and humans to survive the freezing snows, winds and rain of the Maine winters, they needed to be very tough. This said, it should not be thought the average Coon Cat, as these felines were then known, was left to fend for itself unduly. History indicates that Coon Cats were probably given greater care than was afforded to most other cats of the day. In its earliest years of development, when its numbers were small, it was a valuable feline. Once its type was plentiful, its toughness and character were really shaped. For many individuals, survival of the fittest became the name of the game.

## BREED HISTORY

The history of the Maine Coon is divisible into two distinct periods. The first concerns the origins of its type. The second is the period that commenced when the cat fancy hobby arrived in America. From the moment the first cat shows took place, the Coon Cat, as a definable breed, was steadily developed. But little was actually known about its origins. Many stories were mythical. They were based on beliefs of the day handed down by farmers, fishermen and others familiar

### RACOON RELATIVES?

One of the myths about Coon Cats is they were the result of love affairs between shorthaired cats and racoons. As a consequence, the cats inherited a heavy weather-resistant coat as well as dark rings on the tail. The fact is that such hybridisation is impossible. The racoon is a member of the family *Procyonidae* (meaning 'first dogs'), so it could not possibly mate with a cat.

The Maine Coon's full, silky long coat, somewhat evident even on these kittens, is more luxuriant than any of the wild felids whence comes our breeds of domestic cat.

with this cat. Other stories were based on word-of-mouth accounts of people said to have had an involvement with the breed.

### THE VIKING THEORY

It has been suggested that on their many visits to the land they called Vinland (North America), the Vikings took longhaired cats with them. It is speculated that centuries later the descendants of these cats mated with domestic shorthairs taken by the Pilgrims to New England. From their offspring the Coon Cat developed.

As romantic as the theory is,

it has major problems. There are no records that would suggest the Pilgrims saw any cats when they arrived in their new homeland. But a more compelling problem is that there is no evidence to support the view that the Vikings had ever seen a longhaired cat.

If they had, it would most certainly have been taken with them to most European countries they invaded. The fact is that the first documented record of longhaired cats reaching Europe (to Italy from Turkey) cites the date of this event as 1621—centuries after the Viking era had ended.

## BOBCAT BROTHERS?

There is a myth explaining the tufts of hair on the ears of the Coon Cat. Again the cats were finding unusual mates. This time at least it was with other cats—the lynx, *Felis lynx*, or the bobcat, *Felis rufus*. It was said that such felids also gave the Coon Cat its large size. In theory at least, such unions are possible genetically, but from a practical standpoint they are not realistic.

### IN RESPONSE TO NATURE

Another theory of origin is that the Coon Cat developed from shorthaired cats in response to the harsh winter conditions. This might seem plausible but carries little merit. The evolution of a weather-resistant coat happens by a continuum of imperceptible small mutations. The process probably takes thousands of years to effect, at least in warm-blooded animals (i.e. birds and mammals).

Only four of the small wild felids possess longer than typical hair length developed in response to harsh conditions. These are the Pallas cat (*Felis manul*), the European wild cat (*Felis sylvestris*), the lynx (*Felis lynx*), and the bobcat (*Felis rufus*). In none of these is the coat comparable with that of the Maine Coon. This suggests the long hair seen in domestic cats may be useful but is far from ideal for combating severe winter

## THE BIRTH OF THE CAT FANCY

On 13 July 1871, at the Crystal Palace, London, Harrison Weir organised the world's first major cat show. It proved a spectacular success and was quickly followed by many others. The hobby of the cat fancy had begun. Cat fever quickly spread to America, where shows were held in many of the eastern states during the later years of the 1870s.

It was not until 1883 that a really major show was staged in America. It was held in Boston over a two-week period. Interestingly, along with Angoras and numerous Coon Cats, there were also cats said to be Siberian, which are not unlike the Maine Coon. These were not heard of again until recent years.

On 8 May 1895, an Englishman, Mr J T Hyde, organised what was America's largest show to that time. It was held on a blistering hot day in Madison Square Garden in New York City and, like the London show years earlier, was a big hit with visitors. The neuter winner was a female brown tabby Maine Cat called Cosey. The silver collar she won was engraved 'National Cat Show 1895 Won by Cosey.' It is a valuable historical item kept in the Cat Fanciers Association CFA (America's largest cat registry) headquarters.

Major shows continued to be held in Boston and in the years 1897, 1898 and 1899 one of Mrs F R Pierce's Maine Cats, King Max—a brown tabby—was unbeatable. His winning run ended in 1900 when his son Donald defeated him.

## MARIE ANTOINETTE (1755–1793)

In discussing the later years of the 18th century it would be remiss not to mention two stories associated with Marie Antoinette, wife of King Louis XVI of France. It is said she gave Angora cats to the Marquis de Lafayette at the time of the American War of Independence (1775–83). Offspring of these were thought to have been part of the gene pool from which the Maine Cats developed.

The better known story relates to the period of the French Revolution. This was not a good time to be a royal. It is said Marie planned to flee to America aboard the *Sally*, a ship captained by a Samuel or Nathaniel Clough of Wiscasset on the Sheepscot River in Maine. Personal possessions, including her six Persian/Angora cats, were placed aboard the ship. However, the queen was beheaded in 1793 before she could make good her escape. The ship hastily departed and arrived in America, where the cats were said to have been the rootstock of the Coon Cats. Both stories are best taken with a pinch of salt.

conditions. If this is so, it is unlikely the coat was evolved as a response to weather conditions.

The alternative route for a coat change is by a major mutation. This represents a quantum leap. Mutations of this type do not appear to be linked to any need to respond to the environment. They are chance happenings that may or may not prove beneficial to the species. Most are of no benefit. For example, the hairless cat, the Sphynx, was developed from a mutation that appeared in Canada, hardly the most logical place for a cat to develop a hairless coat!

If, however, a mutation created in one region can be transported to a region where it may hold benefit, then its retention is more probable. The benefit may be climatic, because of breeder perception that it will be beneficial, or a combination of both. However, in domestic cats all mutational forms have been transported around the world solely because they were a novelty, or fashionable, thus desirable. This translates to being valuable.

The conclusion that can be drawn from these observations is that the coat of the Maine Coon did not specifically evolve to meet climatic needs. Further, as longhaired cats were present in Europe and the Near East long before they were recorded in

Among the most handsome of domesticated cat breeds, the Maine Coon possesses distinctive characteristics beyond its magnificent coat to make it attract the attention of cat lovers around the world.

America, it would seem reasonable to assume that such cats were imported from these regions.

**PROBABLE BREED ORIGINS**

The arrival of the Persian and Angora cats into Europe during the late 17th century caused quite a sensation. They quickly became very fashionable with both the nobility and the wealthy. It would seem highly probable that by the later years of 18th century examples of these felines would have reached American ports.

By that period the coastline of southern Maine was the centre of a thriving shipbuilding industry,

The brown tabby Maine coon has remained the most popular and distinctive to the present day.

as well as a place of general commerce. Ships were continually leaving the many ports for destinations all over the world. On their return it is inconceivable they would not have brought longhaired cats with them as valued ship's cats or as desirable items of trade.

## THE BOOK OF THE CAT

Possibly the earliest account of the breed in cat books, and still the definitive text on the breed's early years, is that of F R Pierce in Frances Simpson's classic work *The Book of the Cat*. This was published by Cassell & Co in London in 1903. In this work, Pierce, who lived in Maine, states her first cat of this type was obtained in 1861. She relates that at that time they were already well known and claimed their origin predated the memory of the oldest of people.

Pierce states that the Coon or Maine Cats were to be found in all the ports. When they bred, their offspring were given to friends and relatives. By this means, and by the sale of kittens as the type became more numerous, they slowly moved inland to the nearby farming communities. The place names that appear in historical accounts and stories are to be found along the coast that stretches east from Biddeford to Bar Harbor and Frenchman Bay. It can therefore be assumed the

**CAPTAIN COON**

The Maine Coon was originally known as the Coon Cat. It also became known as the Maine Cat or Shag, and only in the 20th century did it become the Maine Coon. We have discussed one explanation why these cats were called Coons, but there is another. It is said a certain sailor, Tom Coon, was in the habit of bringing longhaired cats back from Europe.

His first cats were said to reside on a farm near Biddeford Pool, where his ship often anchored. He continued with this practice after he became a captain. As a consequence the cats became known as 'Coon' cats. A final little story relating to Tom Coon states he was Chinese. In a way this may actually have been true. However, the China referred to is not the country of that name; rather, it is a small town on the south shores of China Lake, near Augusta, Maine.

Coon Cat first arrived, and was developed, in that region.

To all accounts, the brown tabby was the predominating colour pattern, but many others were also evident. Tabbies would have been the most numerous in Europe, thus the most readily available. It is noteworthy that Pierce mentions blue-eyed white examples as being very carefully nursed and obviously more valuable than the tabbies. This points to the Angora and Persian

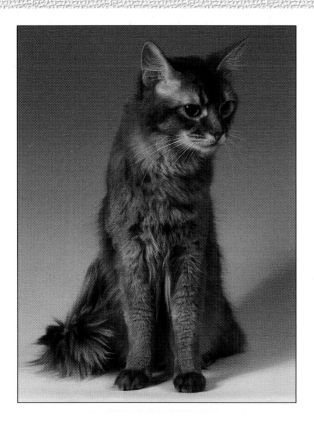

Pierce mentions a Captain Condon as owning a most attractive cream Maine Cat whose kittens were well known for their quality during the 1880s. A Captain Ryan was another breeder. He specialised in blacks, on which he lavished much attention.

## THE BREED EMERGES

By the 1860s it is clear from Pierce's comments that the Maine Cat was very popular, and proud owners held competitions for the best Coon Cat at local fairs. The most notable of these was held at Skowhegan, near Bangor. The top award was for the 'Maine State Champion Coon Cat.' From this period onwards, the Maine Cat begins to emerge as an identifiable type.

During the 1870s, the Maine Cat was continually gaining admirers and its popularity extended well beyond the boundaries of its home state. The future looked very bright. However, an event took place across the Atlantic Ocean that would have an enormous effect on the Maine Cat, as well as on all indigenous cat types of Europe.

## ILL WINDS OF CHANGE

The early years of cat showing in America were good for Coon Cats because many people owned them. But as the 20th century unfurled, matters changed dramat-

as obvious ancestors of the Maine Coon.

In the later years of the 18th century longhaired white cats were especially valued in Europe. They began to appear in family portraits, such as those done by Jean-Jacques Bachelier (circa 1761) and Martin Drolling the Elder (circa 1798). It should be stated that the Persian cats of that period were very similar to the Angora and not like the modern Persians. In those days these two cats were also known as French or Eastern cats.

ically. Wealthy owners developed large catteries and would exhibit 20 or more cats in a show. The top British breeders exported quality Persians and Angoras, which exchanged hands for exceedingly high prices. The Siamese was becoming very fashionable, as were other emerging British and European breeds.

In this high fashion, big dollar and booming new hobby there was little place for a working class cat whose ancestry could not be traced back to some royal, religious or other equally pretentious origins. Visitors at cat shows wanted to see the exotic, not the backwoods or city cats with which they were so familiar. If you wanted success, you had to have the appropriate breeds, and if the stock came from Britain, all the better.

Much after 1911, when a blue Maine Cat was a winner at Portland, the breed was steadily

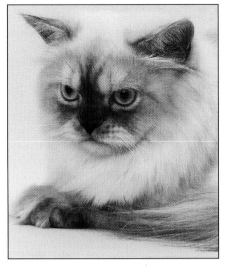

Derived from the Angoras, the Persian cat, shown here as a Colourpoint, represents the earliest breed of longhaired cat known to both Europeans and Americans.

relegated to the 'has beens' of cat history. It lost its championship status with each of the growing number of American registry associations and could only be exhibited in the Any Other Variety classes. These are for the emerging breeds and those on their way out! But it's an ill wind that blows no good, as time was to prove.

## THE MODERN PERIOD

After many years in the feline wilderness, the Maine Cat began what was to be a long comeback road unmatched in feline history. By the 1950s the breed was said to be extinct. This was rather an exaggeration and in 1953 a small group of devotees formed the Central Maine Cat Club, appropriately based in Skowhegan. Through the efforts of this club,

Long hair on cats is the result of a coat mutation, similar to hairlessness. The Sphynx cat, illustrated here, was created by a spontaneous mutation in Canada, a rather cold climate to yield such a shamelessly naked kitty.

It is believe that
the Maine Coon
derived from
Persian and
Angora cats that
arrived to
American ports in
the late 1700s.

shows were held, pedigree records maintained and a breed standard was drafted. American breed registries began accepting the Coon for registration during the 1960s as the breed gained fresh promotion and impetus. The club was disbanded in 1964.

In 1968 the Maine Coon Breeders and Fanciers Association was created by a handful of dedicated Coon breeders. By May 1976 the CFA once again granted breed championship status. In 1985 the governor of Maine accorded the breed a final seal of approval when declaring it to be the Official Cat of the State, a rare honour. The Maine Coon was well and truly back in the ranks of the cat fancy.

**THE BREED IN BRITAIN**
Although the Maine Coon was imported into Mainland Europe during the 1950s, it was not until some years later that it made its appearance in Britain, possibly in the early 1980s. In 1985 the Maine Coon Cat Club was founded to cater to British enthusiasts. When it first gained preliminary show status with the Governing Council of the Cat Fancy (GCCF), the Maine Coon was placed in the Long-hair Section. This housed the Persian, Turkish Van, Balinese and other longhaired breeds.

However, by 1990 it had been transferred to the Foreign Shorthair Section. In this it joined

In 1985, the Maine Coon cat was declared the Official Cat of the State of Maine.

the Ragdoll, Norwegian Forest and Somali. This classification was inappropriate for these breeds. Consequently, in 1993, the GCCF created the Semi-Longhair Section, which is where the Maine Coon and similar hair-length breeds are now housed.

The wheel has certainly gone full circle for this magnificent feline. In the 19th century it lost its appeal because it was too familiar at a time when the hobby wanted the exotic. In an ironic twist of events, the very same fact has been the source of the breed's revival. The Persian and Siamese became so familiar that the Maine Coon and certain other breeds became the exotics! These were the breeds then wanted by the new generation of hobbyists.

The Maine Coon may never reach the dizzying heights achieved in its home country, but is equally as unlikely to fall into the sort of demise it did over one hundred years ago. Its many outstanding virtues have now been proven and it has rightfully become a world-wide favourite.

# A Portrait of the

# MAINE COON CAT

For those not acquainted with pedigreed cats, the Maine Coon appears to be a typical longhaired cat of the type seen the world over, especially in countries that experience cold winters. It is clearly not of the sedate Persian type. Rather, it is an altogether more rugged feline with a coat that would obviously keep its owner warm under cold, harsh conditions. If displaying lynx-like tufts on its ears, there is a wild look to the breed. This is particularly so when its is clothed in the brown tabby pattern with which it is traditionally associated.

To be described as a 'typical' is not derogatory to this breed. Indeed, if it did not have such an appearance, one might question whether its very natural appearance had been changed to meet the whims of fashion, a fate many breeds have suffered. It is a large breed, though not as large as is sometimes claimed. A typical male will weigh 11–16 lbs while the female is lighter at 9–12 lbs. There will always be some cats heavier than the weights given, but these would not be typical of the breed as a whole.

Today the breed is seen in a very extensive range of colours and patterns, but these are not considered to be especially important in a quality Maine Coon. The essence of the breed lies in its conformation, its magnificent coat and its rock-solid temperament.

The definitive description of the Maine Coon is written in its official standard. This is prepared by the breed's national club and presented to a major registration body for adoption. Thereafter it is used as the blueprint for judging the breed in exhibitions run under the rules of the given registry. Although the standard of each national registry will differ somewhat in its wording, its meaning remains the same.

The following description is not that of any one association but is based on reference to three major registries. These are the GCCF of Britain and the CFA and TICA of America. The GCCF is Britain's largest registry while both the American registries are

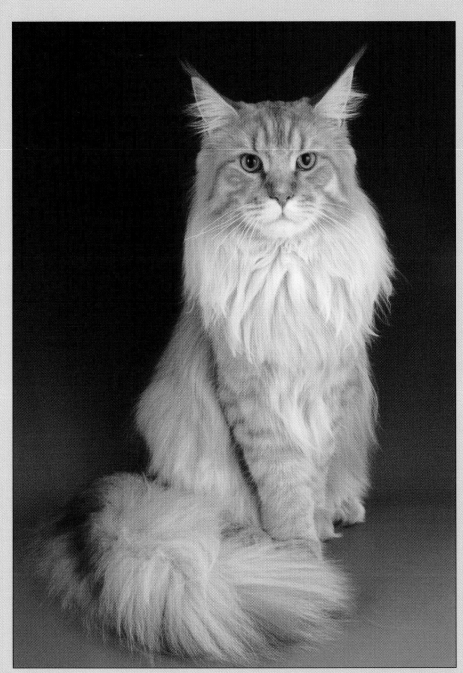

A magnificent red Maine Coon cat displays his frontal ruff, long hair extending from the sides of the head to the chest.

operational in some European countries.

Author comments have been included where these were deemed appropriate. The description should meet the needs of most fanciers. Those planning to breed and/or exhibit should obtain the standard of the association with whom their cats are registered.

It should be added that the only realistic way to fully understand and appreciate a standard is by comparing it with quality Maine Coons at a show. This is essential because a standard is subject to flexibility of interpretation by both breeders and judges. Terms such as 'large,' 'medium,' 'small,' 'long,' 'short' and 'in proportion to' are, in the absence of a yardstick, meaningless.

**Head & Neck:** Head is of medium length with the width being somewhat shorter than the length. In mature males, due allowance should be made for development of jowls, which give the face a fuller, wider look. The muzzle in profile is square, of medium length and blunt. The nose leather and upper lip should lay in the same perpendicular line and continue to form a firm chin. The bite should be level. This means the upper and lower incisor teeth should just touch, neither protruding in front of the other.

When viewed in profile, the nose joins the forehead brow via a gentle concave curve at the nasal bridge.

There should not be a pronounced stop, nor should the

The tortoiseshell pattern exhibits two colours intermingled and only normally occurs on female cats.

The ears of the Maine Coon cat are large, pointed and set high on the head, always exhibiting the characteristic tufts at the tips.

head form a straight line from the brow to the nose tip. The face gives the impression of a wedge, but one in which the lines are gently rounded as compared with the straight lines of the Oriental type. The neck is of moderate length, thick and especially muscular in adult males.

**Ears:** Large, pointed and ideally with tufted tips. The ears are wide at their base and set high on the head with just a slight outward tilt. The distance between them should be no more than the width of the ear base. Ample ear furnishings are often

present—these being the hairs that grow from the ear's open base.

**Eyes:** Large and round when alert, they may become oval when relaxed. Set well apart with their aperture being set slightly oblique towards the outer base of the ear. Colour is a shade of green, gold or copper. There is no relationship between eye and coat colour. Blue or odd-eyed (each eye a different colour) are acceptable in white cats.

**Body:** Of medium to large size, the body is of a rectangle shape and substantial bone. It should by very muscular, with good chest width. The rump has a squared appearance.

**Legs & Feet:** Medium in length, the legs must be substantial and display good bone and ample muscle. The large paws are round and should contain five toes on the front feet and four on the rear. The toes should be tufted with hair, these often being called snowshoes.

Substantial front feet on a Maine Coon with toes well tufted with hair.

**Tail:** This should be at least as long as the body from its shoulders to the tail root. Its base is wide and tapers gradually towards its tip.

**Coat:** The Maine Coon sports both winter and summer coats. The description here is that of the winter coat, the summer being shorter, though the tail largely retains its beautiful length even in the warmer months. In order to provide maximum weather resistance, the coat is comprised of a short but adequate soft underfur that creates warmth. A much more substantial topcoat of smooth silk-like guard hairs protects this from rain, snow and wind. The result is a relatively self-maintaining coat that is easier to groom than might initially be expected.

There is a frontal ruff of long hair that begins on the sides of the head and continues down the chest. The hair on the head, neck and shoulders is short but gets longer on the flanks and back. The fur of the breeches and underbelly is full and described as being shaggy. Tail fur is long and flowing, often parting on either side of the tail. Any tendency towards a woolly or fluffy coat is decidedly undesirable.

**Breed Faults:** Specific breed faults, as opposed to those applicable to any cat, are as follows: Cobby (squared) body, fine bones and lack of good muscle. Lack of size. Long thin legs. Blue or odd-eyed cats in any coat colour other than white. A definite stop or nose break at the nasal bridge. Short or flared ears. Pronounced whisker pads. A coat that has an even length over the whole body. Excess undercoat. Lack of tufts on the paws. Lack of belly fur (shag). The extent of acceptable white fur is discussed where applicable.

Finally, the colours chocolate and lilac, together with the Siamese restriction pattern, which would indicate hybridisation with a breed carrying the genes for this,

# MAINE COON COLOURS

**WHITE**    Pure white with no evidence of yellow or any other colour. Nose leather and paw pads pink.

**BLACK**    A dense coal black. There should be neither evidence of rust colour at the hair tips nor any indication of the smoke pattern, meaning a lighter coloration towards the hair roots. Nose leather black, paw pads black or brown.

**BLUE**    Better described as being a slate blue or blue-grey. Nose leather and paw pads blue.

**RED**    A deep rich colour with no indication of ticking. The intensity of red in pure-bred cats is more pronounced than in typical ginger street cats. Lips and chin should be the same colour as the coat. Nose leather and paw pads brick red. Red is the only sex-linked colour in cats.

**CREAM**    A pale to medium cream or a buff colour. Genes that dilute red create this colour, thus it is sex-linked and its shade is determined by the shade of red the dilution genes are working on. Nose leather and paw pads pink.

are not permitted. In the Cat Fanciers Association of America (CFA), the ticked body pattern of the Abyssinian tabby is also cited as not being acceptable.

## COLOURS & PATTERNS
While the Maine Coon is not available in quite the same number of colours and patterns as breeds such as the Persian, the range is nonetheless impressive. In all, there are over 60 options from which the potential owner can select. In America all the various options are cited in the standards. In the GCCF standard the patterns are named, but not described, nor are the colours

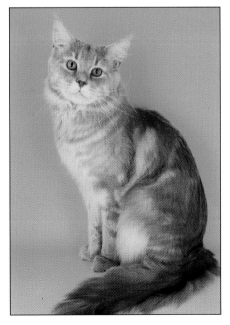

A cream-coloured Maine Coon cat, a colour that is the dilution of red.

cited. However, all colours are acceptable other than those mentioned under breed faults.

### COLOURS

There are five colours to choose from: white, black, blue, red and cream. A cat may carry the colour as a solid, meaning all over its body, or combined with a pattern. When the colour is solid, also known as being a self-colour, it should be the same from the hair roots to the tip with no evidence of shading.

### PATTERNS

There are five basic colour patterns accepted in the Maine Coon. In some instances these are subdivided into variations on the basic pattern. For example, the tabby is a basic pattern, but there are two types of tabby. Likewise, the tipped pattern is divisible into three sub-varieties.

Basic patterns can also be combined to create composites. For example, the tabby may combine with the van pattern to create the van tabby and white. The tabby is by far the most popular pattern, though others are gaining more followers each year.

Some colour pattern combinations may not be readily available. They may require extensive enquiries to locate breeders of them.

A blue-silver tabby Maine Coon cat, exhibiting well-contrasting hues of blue and a majestic, long, well-furred tail.

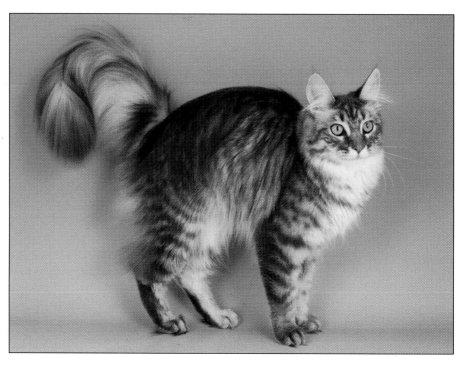

## TABBY

In this pattern there is a distinctive letter 'M' on the forehead. Narrow lines run from this over the crown and down the neck to the shoulders. A central stripe runs from the neck down the back to the tail. Either side of this is a stripe separated from it by the ground colour.

Mascara lines extend from the corner of the eyes and pass over the cheeks, eventually coming together. The neck and chest are ringed with necklaces, while the legs are ringed with bracelets. The tail is evenly ringed. This pattern is applicable to either of the two tabby varieties, mackerel and classic or blotched, which differ only in their body markings.

In the tabby colours, the name refers to the ground colour. The markings will be a darker shade of this and should display good contrast to it. In the brown and silver varieties, the markings are black. The most popular tabby colour is brown, which is a copper colour. The other colours are silver, blue, blue-silver, red and cream. The tabby pattern can also be combined with certain other patterns to create varieties such as the tortie tabby. In turn, these can be combined with white to provide even more options.

## BICOLOUR

This is a combination of a solid colour and white. The CFA requires that the colour should predominate: white areas should be located on the face, chest, belly, legs and feet. The GCCF requires that the coat should exhibit not more than one-third white. This pattern is available in black, blue, red and cream.

## VAN

This pattern was derived from the Turkish Van breed, native to the area around Lake Van. The coat is predominately white. Colour is located on the head, though it must not extend below the eyes or beyond the back of the ears. The head colour should be separated by a white blaze. The tail is coloured and may display faint rings. It may also extend a little way up the back. Sometimes small irregularly placed blotches (thumbprints) of colour may appear on the body. Though not desirable, they are acceptable. The colour may be any of the solids as well as tabby in the various colours.

## TIPPED

This is created by the action of inhibitor genes that restrict the amount of pigment along the hair shaft. There are three varieties of this very pretty pattern: smoke, shaded and shell. In each case the base of the hair shaft is white, or as near to this as possible, while the rest of the shaft is pigmented. This may be with any of the various solid colours.

# MAINE COON TABBY VARIETIES

| | |
|---|---|
| CLASSIC or BLOTCHED TABBY | This pattern is characterised by large oyster-shaped blotches on the flanks, which are surrounded by swirls. Viewed from above, there should be a butterfly-wing pattern on the shoulders. Ideally, both sides of the body should have identical bold markings. |
| MACKEREL TABBY | This is the wild-type tabby in which narrow stripes extend vertically down to the underbelly from each of the lines next to the central back stripe. The more stripes there are the better, and they should be unbroken. This pattern is often commonly known as the tiger pattern in America. |

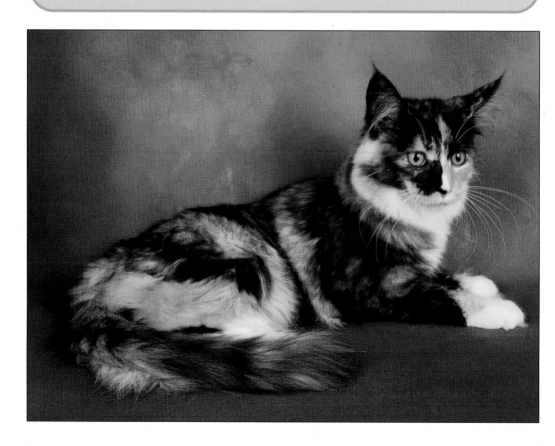

# MAINE COON
## TIPPED PATTERN VARIETIES

| VARIETY | DESCRIPTION | COLOUR CHOICE |
| --- | --- | --- |
| SMOKE | In this variety the pigment extends almost to the hair roots. In repose the cat looks a solid colour. But as soon as it moves, the hairs part and the light undercolour is seen. It creates a subtle contrasting effect. | Black, blue, red (also called cameo), cream, tortoiseshell and blue-cream. |
| SHADED | Here the pigment extends about one-third down the shaft. The effect is to create shades of colour and white, the more so when the cat is on the move. | Silver (where the tipping is black), red (cameo), cream or pewter (which is similar to silver but darker). |
| SHELL | This tipping is the most delicate, being restricted to the very ends of the hair. The effect is of a white cat dusted with sparkling colour. | Red (also known as red chinchilla), cream and silver or chinchilla (where the tips are black). |

### TORTOISESHELL
This pattern is unusual in two ways. One is because the sex of the cat has a bearing on what the colour will be (the pattern is said to be sex-linked). The second aspect is that two solid colours appear together. The pattern, and its dilute form, the blue-cream, is a female-only variety (other than in aberrant males).

Colours are normally inherited via body chromosome cells, but in the case of red it is carried on the sex chromosomes. One of these is designated X, the other Y. A male cat is XY, a female XX. The Y chromosome is concerned only with matters of gender. The colour red has the

*Opposite page: A rarely seen colour variety of the Maine Coon is the tortoiseshell smoke.*

1,4   1,6   2,4   3,5   1,6   1,6   3,4   1,4

FROM THE ATLAS OF FELINE ANATOMY FOR VETERINARIANS BY HUDSON/HAMILTON. COURTESY OF W. B. SAUNDERS COMPANY.

## PARTICOLOURED CAT

Not a new breed of feline, this 'particoloured cat' illustrates the many possibilities of the feline coat. Since cats come in three basic hair lengths, short, long and rex (curly), all three coat lengths are illustrated here. Additionally, different coat patterns, such as mackerel tabby, Abyssinian and self-coloured, are depicted to demonstrate the differences.

**1—3 COAT TYPES**
  **1** Shorthair coat
  **2** Rex (curly) coat
  **3** Longhair coat

**4—6 COAT COLOUR PATTERNS**
  **4** Mackerel (tabby)
  **5** Abyssinian
  **6** Self-coloured

# SKIN AND HAIRCOAT OF CATS

Schematic illustration of histologic layers of the integument skin.

A Epidermis
B Dermis
C Subcutis

7 Primary hair
8 Secondary hairs
9 Area of sebaceous gland
10 Apocrine sweat gland
11 M arrector pili
12 Nerve fibre
13 Cutaneous vessels
14 Tactile hair
15 Fibrous capsule
16 Venous sinus
17 Sensory nerve fibres
18 External root sheath
19 Hair papilla

Schematic illustration of a tactile hair (whisker).

A female Maine Coon cat in an attractive tipped patterned coat.

The tabby pattern is the one most people identify with the Maine Coon cat, although it may one day be eclipsed by the rainbow of other colour possibilities.

The green eyes on this Maine Coon make the white coloration a very dramatic choice for the breed.

genetic symbol of O for orange. A lower case o indicates non-red.

This means that a male can either be red, XOY or non-red XoY (meaning any other colour such as blue, black and so on). However, a female can be XOXO, which is red, XoXo, which is non-red, or XOXo, which is red and non-red in the same coat. In America it is preferred that the red and non-red (black or blue) be located in clearly defined patches, thus the term patched.

In Britain it is preferred the two colours are intermingled, except on the head where a blaze of one colour is permissible. The tortoiseshell can be combined with white and with other patterns, such as the tabby, which creates the torbie. There are potentially many combinations and these can be seen in either black or red or blue and cream (blue-cream).

Although many colour patterns can look quite stunning, the singular drawback of this, depending on your views, is that a few of these may one day eclipse the tabby in popularity. This situation has happened in other long-established 'natural' breeds once they have gained very high popularity. It is to be hoped the tabby always remains a popular variety because it is so strongly associated with the Maine Coon. More than any other pattern, it gives the breed its natural rugged beauty.

## EYE COLOUR

Eye colours in cats are determined based on the amounts of brown-black and yellow-red pigments in the eye. The rainbow of eye colours spans blue, green and copper, including all the various shades of these three colours. Many cats have eyes that appear blue and/or green, though there are no such pigments in the feline eye. These colours appear as 'optical illusions' known as the Tyndall Phenomenon that involves light waves. To create blue

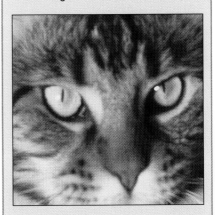

eyes, the dark pigment in the eyes absorbs the light rays and the effect is blue. Green eyes are created by light passing through yellow pigment, allowing blue rays to be reflected; the combination of colours creates the illusion of green.

Copper eyes in cats are more straightforward and are created by brown pigments modified by yellow or black, thus creating hazel, copper, orange and various shades of these darker colours.

# Purchasing a

# MAINE COON CAT

## THE PURCHASING PROCESS

Never rush into the purchase of a companion that is to be given the freedom of your home and will become an integral part of your life. A pure-bred cat may live 20 or more years. This is a long time. It is very prudent to take all those steps that will minimise the chances of your ever regretting the choice you make. Once you have decided on the sex, age, reason for purchase (pet, show or breeding) and desired colour pattern, proceed cautiously, heeding all the advice given here. By following a planned process of selection, you will also gain much useful information.

It is no wonder the Maine Coon Cat is so popular. Before the decision to purchase is made, however, careful consideration should be given to the implications and responsibilities of cat ownership. If more owners would do this, there would be far fewer half-starved pets roaming our streets or having to live in local animal-rescue centres.

### OWNER RESPONSIBILITY

The initial cost of a Maine Coon Cat represents only a fraction of its lifetime's cost. The first question is, 'Can you afford one?' The kitten needs vaccinations to protect it against various diseases. Boosters are then required every year. Cat food is more costly than that for dogs. There is also the cost of cat litter every week. Periodic vet checks and treatment for illness or accidents must be allowed for. When holidays are taken, you may need to board the pet at a cattery.

From the outset there will be additional costs apart from that of the kitten. It will need a basket, carrying box, feeding and grooming utensils, scratching post and maybe a collar and a few toys. If you have any doubts at all about being able to supply all these needs, it is best not to obtain a cat.

Other matters also need careful thought. If you are planning to have a family, will your love for the Maine Coon be maintained once a baby arrives? Cats are generally not a problem with family newcomers, providing they are not ignored or treated as being a threat to the baby. Never purchase a kitten for a child unless you want one yourself. If you are elderly, it is only fair to consider what would happen to your cherished pet if it were to outlive you or if you were to become hospitalised for long periods.

It is most unfortunate that many people rush into the purchase of cats on impulse. They then find they cannot cope when problems, and extra costs, ensue. Some lose interest in the pet once it matures past its kitten stage. The evidence of these realities is easily seen in the growing number of cats abandoned or taken to animal shelters every year. Invariably their owners will make feeble excuses for why the cat cannot be kept. But the bottom line is they did not stop to consider at the outset what responsible ownership entailed.

The Maine Coon is an ideal choice for those wanting a pure-

## DOCUMENTATION

When you take delivery of your kitten, certain paperwork should come with it:

1. Three- to five-generation pedigree.
2. Breeder-signed registration application form or change of owner registration form. This assumes the breeder has registered stock. If they have not, the kitten cannot be registered at a later date. It is worth less than the kitten with registration paperwork. You are not recommended to purchase a kitten from unregistered parents.
3. Certificates of health, vaccination and neutering, if this has been effected. Ideally, it is desirable that the kitten's parents have been tested negative for major diseases. Additionally, the breeder should know the blood group of your kitten. This may be of importance at a later date.
4. Details of worming or other treatments attended.
5. Diet sheet, feeding timetable and brand names of food items used. This diet should be maintained for at least ten days while the kitten adjusts to the trauma of moving home.
6. Signed receipt for monies paid.
7. Signed copy of any guarantees. Not all breeders give a guarantee on the reasonable grounds that once the kitten leaves their care, its onward well-being is no longer under their control.

## TAKING KITTY HOME

Arrange collection of the kitten as early in the day as possible. If a long journey is involved, be sure to take a few breaks so kitty does not suffer from travel sickness. Do not make stops to show the kitten to friends; this represents a health hazard. Once home, offer the kitten a drink, then allow it to sleep if it so requires. Children must be educated to handle a kitten gently, never to tease it and to respect its sleeping privacy. Until it is litter-trained it should be restricted to the kitchen or another room with an easy-to-clean floor surface.

bred longhaired cat, yet one that has retained a very natural, no-nonsense feline disposition. It is a physically agile cat but does not use its energy in a wasteful manner. As a kitten, like those of any breed, it will clamber up and over everything in sight when playing.

However, even before it matures, such strenuous activities become less frequent. It will then have occasional moments of madness, but generally will be very well mannered and sedate without ever being quite as laid-back as a Persian. This does not suggest it stops playing.

Its natural hunting instincts are never far below the surface, but its exercise is more restricted to ground-level activities rather than climbing. Ornaments on shelves and expensive curtains are generally much safer with this breed than with those that are hyperactive.

The Maine Coon has a low threshold for stalking and hunting, as would be expected of a breed developed from hardy working cats. This means it takes little to prompt these cats to hunt rodents, birds or any other prey species. The Maine Coon is therefore a good mouser. However, on the downside, it may take its toll on the local bird population if given outdoor freedom.

Perhaps surprisingly for such a large breed, the Maine Coon is not a vocal pest as are some Oriental breeds. Generally, its vocalisations are restricted to soft chirps and equally soft meows. However, when needed, these cats can attract your attention with a voice on par with their size.

The Maine Coon will have no difficulty in living in a family unit that includes children and other animals. The breed's reliable temperament allows it to cope with most situations. The Maine Coon also displays a degree of independence. This reflects in the fact that while it adores human attention it does not pester to gain this.

All in all, the breed is very definitely one that will satisfy a wide cross-section of potential owners. It is lively and affectionate and possesses a predictably solid feline nature. It displays just enough independence to remind its owner it is still a very natural feline.

## KITTEN OR ADULT?

Most potential owners normally want a kitten because it is so cute, cuddly and playful. A kitten is easily trained and has not yet developed bad habits, which the older Maine Coon may have done. This said, if you plan to breed or exhibit, there are advantages in obtaining a young adult. Other potential owners, such as the

**HOMEMADE TOYS**
Cats love to play and pet shops have many cat toys to choose from. Sometimes, however, people give their cats homemade toys. These can be harmful to your cat, as they could have pieces that could break off and be swallowed. Only give your pet toys from the pet shop that have been proven safe for cats.

elderly, may benefit by avoiding the demanding needs of a young kitten. In both of these instances, a good age is when the youngster is 9–15 months old. Even a fully mature Maine Coon may prove an excellent choice for some owners.

Kittens should not be obtained under 12 weeks old, though 14–16 weeks is better. No reputable breeder will sell them younger than this. Less caring breeders will let them go to new homes as young as eight weeks of age. Such juveniles

## A HEALTHY KITTEN

Closely inspect any kitten before making a final decision. Keep in mind the following points:

**Eyes and nose:** Clean and clear with no signs of discharge.
**Ears:** Fresh-smelling and erect.
**Coat:** Healthy, not dull or dry.
**Anal region:** Clean with no staining of the fur.
**Feet:** Four toes on each foot, plus a dewclaw on the inside of each front leg.
**Teeth:** Correct bite.

There should be no signs of parasites or bald areas of fur. A potbelly may indicate worms.

will barely have been weaned. They will not have developed the needed resistance to major diseases. They are more likely to become stressed by the premature removal from their mother and siblings. Their vaccinations will not be fully effective. These facts will dramatically increase the risk of immediate problems.

**SEX & COLOUR PATTERN**
If it is to be purely a pet, the Maine Coon's gender is unimportant. Both are delightful. Males are usually larger, bolder and more outgoing. Females tend to be more discerning about which humans they like. However, each Maine Coon is an individual. Its character and health, more than its sex, should be the basis of selection. Again, the sex is unimportant for the potential exhibitor. It is not even necessary for the cat to be sexually 'entire.' Classes for neuters are featured in shows.

Those with breeding aspirations are advised to obtain only females. All pet owners should regard neutering (males) and spaying (females) as obligatory. Today this can be effected at any age after eight weeks.

The colour pattern is a matter of personal preference. It should never be placed ahead of health and character. Some colours and patterns will be more readily available than others will. The more popular varieties may be less costly than the rarer ones. This would generally not apply to prospective breeding or exhibition individuals where type quality will be as important as colour or pattern.

## LOOK BEFORE YOU LEAP

It is important that you view as many Maine Coon kittens as you can. This gives you a good mental picture of what a healthy typical example should look like and cost for the quality and colour you want. Normally, you will get what you pay for. If you look for the cheapest kitten, there will be a sound reason why it is the cheapest!

The best place to start your search is a cat show. At these, most of the colour varieties will be on display. Purchase the show catalogue. It lists all the exhibitors and their addresses. You can see if any live in your immediate locality. Whenever possible, it is best to purchase locally so you can visit the home of the breeder. Some will insist you do so in order to be satisfied that you will make a good owner.

Shows and breeders are advertised in the various cat magazines available from

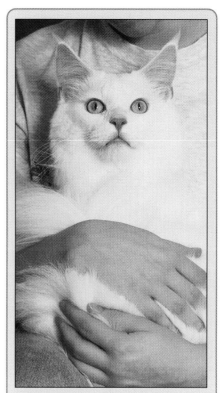

## ADOPTING AN ADULT

Some owners, such as the elderly, may benefit by adopting an adult cat. They can avoid the demanding needs of a young kitten and enjoy the advantages of a well-trained adult, making grooming an easier task. Breeders and exhibitors can also benefit from purchasing an older cat because it is easier to assess the quality. Sometimes, though, older cats can have bad habits that are hard to break. So if you are thinking about obtaining an older cat, it is important to thoroughly investigate possible behavioural and health problems.

Selecting a kitten from a litter of Maine Coon darlings like this one would be quite a task. Many breeders still believe that the kitten will choose its own owner, an adage that gains particular weight with the discerning Maine Coon breed.

newsagents. You can also contact a major cat registry. They will supply a list of national and regional clubs, which are usually able to supply breeder lists. When visiting a breeder, always make an appointment. Try to visit no more than one a day. This reduces the risk that you may transport pathogens (disease-causing organisms) from one establishment to the next. Selecting a good breeder is a case of noting the environment in which the cats are kept, the attitude of the owner to you and their cats, and how friendly and healthy the kittens look. It is vital the chosen kitty has an outgoing personality. It must not appear timid or very shy. This indicates a lack of breeder socialisation or a genetic weakness in its temperament. Either way, it is not a kitten you should select.

**CHOOSING A KITTEN**
If you choose the breeder wisely, and especially if a friend recommends him, this will remove potential problems related to your making a poor choice. However, a little knowledge on what to look for will not go amiss. Observe the kittens from a distance to ensure none is unduly lethargic, which is never a good sign. If any display signs of illness, this should bring to an end any

further thoughts of purchase from that source. A reputable breeder would not allow an ill kitten to remain within its litter.

It is always advisable to select a kitten that shows particular interest in you. Maine Coons are very discerning. If both of you are drawn to each other, this will greatly enhance the bonding essential for a strong relationship.

Once a particular kitten has been selected, it should be given a close physical inspection. The eyes and nose must show no signs of weeping or discharge. The ears will be erect and fresh-smelling. The coat should look healthy, never dry and dull. There must be no signs of parasites in the fur. There will be no bald areas of fur, nor bodily swellings or abrasions. Lift the tail and inspect the anal region. This must be clean, with no indication of congealed faecal matter. Any staining of the fur indicates current or recent diarrhoea.

The kitten must not display a potbelly. This may indicate worms or other internal disorders. Check the teeth to be sure of a correct bite. Bear in mind that the jawbones do not develop at the same rate. Minor imperfections may correct themselves (they may also get worse), but major faults will not. Inspect the feet to see that there are four toes on each, plus a dewclaw on the inside of each front leg.

With respect to the colour, there is no link between this and health other than deafness in certain white varieties. Any faults in the colour or its evenness will only be of importance in breeding or exhibition individuals. The potential breeder/exhibitor should obtain a copy of the official standard so he is *au fait* with all colour, pattern, and bodily faults of the breed.

## CAT LITTER

The litter that is used in cat boxes can be very variable, and in many cases cats reject the use of a cat box because of the litter. Certainly, if your cat rejects the use of the cat box, you should try different litters. You can start with the litters available at your local pet shop, then you can try sand, dirt, cedar shavings or whatever will appeal to your cat. Several cat owners grow clover in a tray and their cats seem to prefer that. However, the tray is kept outdoors and the cats may simply be marking the clover tray rather than using it for elimination purposes.

Cat toys are entertaining for cat and owner alike. Purchase toys that require interaction between you and your Maine Coon, thereby affording the cat exercise and companionship while playing.

Liners are available for most litter trays to assist in keeping them clean and more manageable.

Cat carriers are a necessity of cat ownership, and no cat welcomes the opportunity of being carted about in a crate. Nonetheless, the carrier is the only safe option for transport to the veterinary surgeon.

Purchasing a scratching post is a smart option for the cat owner. It's best to purchase a sturdy, well-made post that will last your cat years of use.

Double-bowl feeders are very convenient for feeding your cat. Go to your pet shop to purchase top-quality feeders, which should come in a variety of colours, styles and sizes.

If you are considering walking your Maine Coon, you must have a lead that is suitable for a cat.

## KITTY SHOPPING SPREE

Certain accessories should be regarded as obligatory and obtained before the kitten arrives in your home.

### SCRATCHING POST

This will save the furniture from being abused! There are many models, some being simple posts, while others are combined with play stations and sleeping quarters. These are the best.

### LITTER BOX(ES)

Some are open trays; others are domed to provide extra privacy. Still others have special bases in which odour removers are fitted.

*Introduce the kitten to the carrier so that he doesn't fear the sight of it the first time you need to use it.*

### CAT LITTER

There are numerous types on the market, each offering advantages and drawbacks. Avoid the low-cost types that contain a lot of dangerous dust. Use those that are fully biodegradable.

### FOOD/WATER DISHES

Polished metal has the longest wear life. Earthenware is less costly than metal and superior to the plastic types.

### GROOMING TOOLS

These will comprise a good-quality bristle brush, a fine-toothed comb, nail trimmers, and a soft chamois leather.

### CAT COLLAR AND/OR HARNESS

Select elasticised collars. Be sure a name and address disc or barrel is fitted to this. A harness must be a snug but comfortable fit if it is to be effective.

### CAT-CARRYING BOX

Essential for transporting the cat to the vet or other places, as well as for home restriction when needed. Be sure it is large enough to accommodate a fully-grown Maine Coon, not just a kitten. The choice is between collapsible models, soft plastic types and, the best choice, those made of fibreglass.

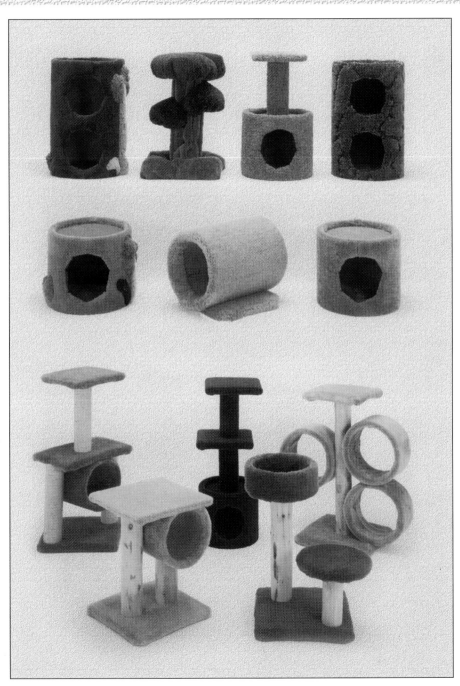

Your local pet shop should have an array of scratching posts that will delight your Maine Coon. Do not attempt to make a post yourself as many carpets are too weak to stand the tearing or may have been dyed with chemicals harmful to cats.

## THE TRAVELLING CAT

Whenever your cat needs to be taken on a car journey, never let it travel loose in the vehicle, which is illegal. It must always be in its carrying box. If a cat were to go under the clutch or brake pedal when the car was moving, this would be dangerous to all occupants. A cat might also spring from one seat to another, which might distract the driver. This could have disastrous results.

Never leave a cat alone in a car on a hot day. The temperature can rise dramatically to the point that the cat is unable to breathe. It could die of heat stroke. Always leave a window partially open, but not so wide that the agile cat could escape.

For a kitten, a human environment holds many dangers. Its owner must protect it from these until it becomes agile and wiser. The following dangers lurk in typical households. Always check whether there are additional ones in your home. The most important decision you need to make from the outset is whether or not the kitten is to be given outdoor liberty.

### HOW MUCH FREEDOM?

More than at any time in the past, the question of how much freedom a cat should be given is the subject of heated debate. It is a very subjective matter. Here the more pertinent points are given so you can relate these to your home location. This, to a very large degree, should influence your decision.

Cats living in or close to an urban area are at the highest safety risk. The amount of traffic is such that death from road accidents is a major concern. In such environments there are high dog populations, some of which are feral. Injury or death from dog

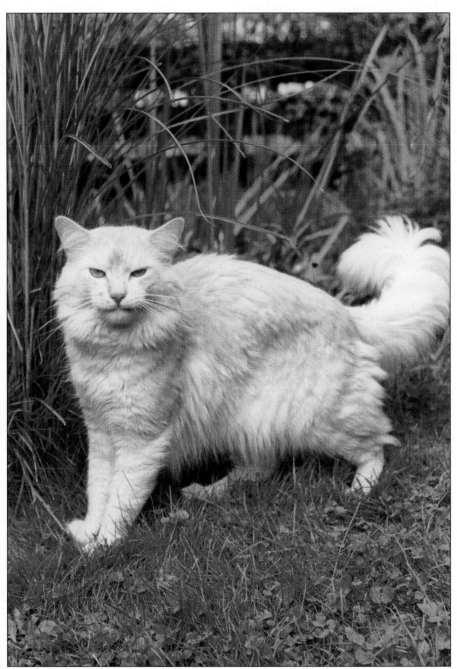

Granting your Maine Coon outdoor freedom is a very personal choice. While the cat will enjoy the excitement of the great outdoors, there are many uncontrollable dangers for a cat to face outside the home.

**BE ONE JUMP AHEAD**
Seemingly innocuous things, such as
doors, can become life-threatening
should they suddenly slam shut on a
kitten due to a strong draught. When
windows and external doors are open,
be sure internal doors are secured with
a doorstop. At all times be one jump
ahead of a kitten in terms of identifying dangerous situations.

attacks is therefore another major
source of danger to a feline.

Urban cat populations are also
extremely high. Far too many cats
are living a virtually feral
existence. These are tough, street-
wise cats that often carry fleas and
other parasites that are vectors of
disease. Some will be carriers of,
or infected with, feline leukaemia
and other deadly diseases.

The typical feline family pet
can be badly injured if it becomes
engaged in fights with these
roaming bullies. Furthermore,
their very presence in and around
a gentle cat's garden can cause the
pet severe stress. This can make it
fearful of stepping outside its
home. In some instances, it may
cause the pet to actually leave its
home.

Sadly, if these risks are not
enough, there is no shortage of
people who will steal a pedigreed
cat, the more so if it is friendly.
Add to this the number of abusive
people who do not like cats
roaming into their gardens, and
the scenario is not good. Finally,
free-roaming cats also take a
heavy toll on local bird and
wildlife populations.

Taking these various facts into
account, the urban cat is best kept
indoors. It can enjoy the benefit of
the outdoors if supplied with a
roomy aviary-type exercise pen.
Some cats can be trained to walk
on a lead. This allows outdoor
enjoyment, even if this is
restricted to the garden. When
walking your cat in public places,
use only a harness. This is much
safer than a collar.

In contrast to urban situations,
the cat living in a rural environment is far safer, the more so if
there are no immediate
neighbours or busy roads. Even
so, it is wise to restrict the cat's
outdoor freedom to daylight

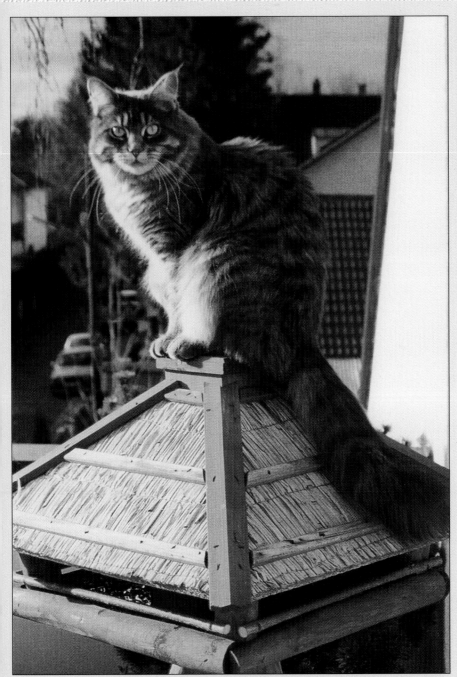

Maine Coons are territorial cats, and like most other cats prefer a higher vantage point to view their surroundings. This Maine Coon is the king of his neighbourhood.

## THE GARAGE AND SHED

These two buildings are very dangerous to a kitten. Sharp and heavy tools, nails, glass jars, garden weed killers and open tins of paint are but a sampling of the items the average family uses or stores in these. A kitten may clamber into the engine compartment of a vehicle. This could be fatal if the owner happened to start the engine before the kitten had removed itself. Always know where the kitten is.

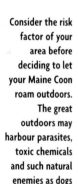

hours. During the night it is more likely to get run over or to threaten local wildlife.

Those living between the extremes of isolated areas and busy urban environments should consider the local risk factor. Generally, it is best to keep the cat indoors but to provide an outdoor exercise pen.

### HOUSEHOLD DANGERS

Within its home, a kitten is best viewed as an accident waiting to happen! The most dangerous room is the kitchen. Hot electric hobs, naked flames from gas rings, boiling pans of food or water and sinks full of water are obvious hazards. An iron left on its board with cable trailing to the floor is an invitation to a kitten to jump up—with potentially fatal consequences. Washing machines or spin dryers with warm clothes in them, and

Consider the risk factor of your area before deciding to let your Maine Coon roam outdoors. The great outdoors may harbour parasites, toxic chemicals and such natural enemies as dogs and other cats.

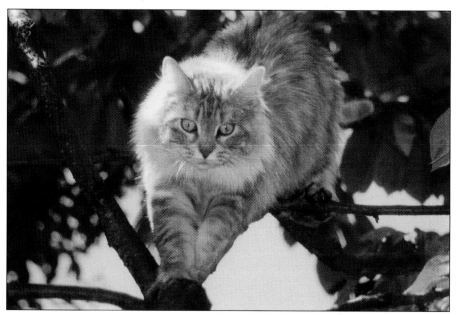

Cats are naturally blest with the ability to climb and nothing challenges that ability like a tree. The expression, 'a cat up a tree' certainly reminds us of the dangers in store for adventure-seeking climbers.

their doors open, are inviting places to nap. Always check that the kitty isn't inside if the door has been left open. Cupboards containing poisonous or other dangerous substances should always be kept securely closed.

In the living room, the normal dangers are aquariums without hoods, unguarded fires, electric bar heaters, poisonous indoor plants, trailing electrical wires and ornaments that may be knocked over by a mischievous kitty. Toilets can be fatal to an over-curious kitten. The same is true of a bath containing water. Balconies should be safeguarded to remove the potential for the kitten to slip and fall.

## OTHER DANGERS
Other potential dangers are when electric tools are left lying about and connected to power outlets—even worse if they are left on, as with bench saws. If the kitten is given freedom to exercise in a garden containing a pond, the kitten must be under constant supervision. Cherished ornaments should be placed out of reach of the kitten, as much for their safety as for any danger they may present to the kitty. It's not always the direct danger of something that can be the problem. If an ornament or similar item crashes to the floor, this can startle the kitten into a panicked departure! The kitten could then fall from a shelf in its haste.

Today the feeding of cats has been reduced to its most simple level with the availability of many scientifically prepared commercial diets. However, this fact can result in owners' becoming casual in their approach to the subject.

## DIETARY DIFFERENCES BETWEEN CATS AND DOGS

You should never feed your cat dog food because dogs and cats have different dietary needs. Cats have a much higher need for fats than dogs, and kittens need more than adult cats. Cats also require unusually high levels of dietary protein as compared with those required by dogs. The foods you choose for your cat must supply these essential components.

While the main object of a given diet is to provide the ingredients that promote healthy growth and maximum immunity to disease, it also fulfils an important secondary role.

A proper diet must maintain in the cat a psychological feeling of well-being that avoids nutritionally related stress problems or syndromes. By ensuring the diet is balanced, of good variety and never monotonous, these dual roles will be achieved. This approach will also avoid the situation of the cat's becoming a finicky eater.

### BALANCE AND VARIETY

A balanced diet means one that contains all of the major ingredients—protein, fats, carbohydrates, vitamins and minerals—in the ratios needed to ensure maximum growth and health. Variety means supplying foods in a range of forms that will maintain and stimulate the cat's interest in its meals. Commercially formulated foods come in three levels of moisture: low (dried), semi-moist and moist (tinned foods).

Generally, the dried and moist forms are more popular. Dried cat foods have the advantage that they can be left in the cat dish for longer periods of time than tinned foods. They are ideal for supplying on a free-choice basis. Like the tinned varieties, they come in a range of popular flavours.

In order to meet the specific needs of a kitten, there are specially formulated foods available. These contain the higher protein levels needed by a growing kitten. As it grows, the

## MILK AND CATS

Milk, although associated with cats, is not needed once kittenhood has passed. Indeed, excess can create skeletal and other problems. Some cats may become quite ill if given too much. They are unable to digest its lactose content. However, small amounts may be appreciated as a treat. Goat's milk, diluted condensed milk and low-lactose milks are better than cow's milk

## MEET THE MEAT-EATERS

Since cats are carnivorous, their teeth are designed to bite and cut. Except for crunching dried foods, cats do very little chewing. They have the fewest teeth of any common domestic mammal— typically 30 (although there are some variations). The canines usually are more developed than the incisors.

kitten can be slowly weaned onto the adult types. There are also special brands available from vets for any kitten or cat that may have a dietary problem as well as special diets for the older cat. These may need lower ratios of certain ingredients, such as proteins and sodium, so as to reduce the workload of the liver.

## IMPORTANT DON'TS

- Do not let your cat become a fussy eater. Cats are not born fussy but are made that way by their owners. Your cat will not starve if given the correct food, but it may try to convince you otherwise. However, a cat that refuses all foods offered may be ill. Contact your vet.
- Do not give a cat sweet and sticky foods. These provide no benefit and, if eaten, will negatively affect normal appetite for wholesome foods.
- Do not feed vitamin and mineral supplements to either kittens or adults unless under advice from a veterinary surgeon. Excess vitamins and minerals can be as bad for your cat's health as a lack of them. They will create potentially dangerous cellular metabolic imbalances.
- Do not give any questionable foods, such as those that smell or look 'off'. If in doubt, discard them. Always store foods in cool, darkened cupboards. Be sure all foods from the freezer and refrigerator are fully thawed.

Flavours should be rotated so that interest in meals is maintained. This also encourages familiarity with different tastes. Naturally, Maine Coon cats will display a greater liking for certain flavours and brands than for others.

### FRESH FOODS

To add greater variety and interest, there are many fresh foods that Maine Coon enjoy. Some will be very helpful in cleaning the teeth and exercising jaw muscles. All have the benefit of providing different textures and smells that help stimulate the palate. Feed these foods two or three times a week as treats or occasionally as complete meals.

Cooked poultry, including the skin, but minus the bones, is usually a favourite, as is quality raw or cooked mincemeat. Cooked beef on the bone gives the cat something to enjoy. Cooked white fish, as well as tinned tuna or sardines, is an example of an ocean delight. Never feed raw fish; this can prove dangerous, even fatal. Although cats rarely enjoy items such as rice, pasta or cooked vegetables, these can, nonetheless, be finely chopped and mixed with meats or fish. Some Maine Coons may develop a taste for them. Various cheeses and scrambled or boiled eggs will often be appreciated—but never give raw eggs.

If the diet is balanced and varied, the addition of vitamin and mineral supplements is unnecessary and can actually prove dangerous. While certain of these compounds are released from the body if in excess, others are not. They are stored and can adversely affect efficient metabolism. If a cat shows loss of condition and disinterest in its food, discuss its diet with a vet.

## HOW MUCH TO FEED

Food intake is influenced by many factors. These are the cat's age, activity level, the ambient

### HIGH-QUALITY FOOD

The value of a cat food is determined by its protein/carbohydrate compositions. High-quality foods will contain more protein. The cat is a prime predator and needs a high proportion of protein in its diet.

### DRIED FOOD— MORE WATER

If the cat is only given dried foods, it is essential that its water bowl is always full; it will need to drink more. But it is best to give both dried and moist food types. This minimises the risk of urological problems created by pH alkalinity associated with dried diets.

temperature (more is eaten in the colder months), the cat's breeding state (rearing kittens) and the quality of the food. Always follow the breeder's recommendations on diet until your kitten has settled into your home. Thereafter the needed quantity will increase as the kitten gets older, until full maturity at about two to three years of age.

As a basic guide, a four-month-old kitten will require four meals a day. At six months old, one meal can be dropped. By twelve months of age, only two meals will be required, possibly only one if dried foods are also available on a free-choice basis.

place its head into deep food
dishes nor do they like their
whiskers to touch the inner
walls. Ensure dishes are wide
and shallow.

**WHERE AND WHEN TO FEED**
Usually, the best place to feed a
cat is in the kitchen. It is

As the number of meals is
decreased, the quantity must be
increased at the others.

**FOOD AND WATER
CONTAINERS**
Maine Coon cats are not too
fussy over what vessels are
used for supplying their food
and water, but a few tips are
useful. Maine Coons do not
like to eat from dirty dishes
any more than you would. The
food bowl should be washed
after each meal. Water
containers should be washed
and replenished every day.
Saucers make ideal food plates.
Wide feeders from your pet
shop are excellent for dried
biscuits. Pot or polished metal
containers are better buys than
plastic. They last longer and
are easier to keep clean.

Having a blunt muzzle, the
Maine Coon does not like to

important to place food and
water dishes as far away from
the litter tray as possible. This
could otherwise deter the cat
from eating. Cats also like to
eat in quiet comfort. Meals
should be spread across the
entire day. When the number of
meals is reduced to two, these
should be given in the morning
and evening at convenient
times. For the Maine Coon
given outdoor freedom, it is
best to feed the main meal in
the evening. This encourages it
to come home at this time. It
can then be kept indoors
overnight.

Once you have
taken on the
responsibility for
a Maine Coon's
life, you must
provide it with
top-quality food.
Follow your vet's
advice and be
aware that as
your cat ages, its
diet will change.

# *Grooming Your*

# MAINE COON CAT

## HAIR, HAIR EVERYWHERE!

Cat's hairs grow denser on the abdomen than on the back. The hairs grow according to both light periodicity (daylight versus dark nights) and temperature. Outdoor cats living in colder climates cast their coats twice a year, in the spring and fall, while house cats do so all year long.

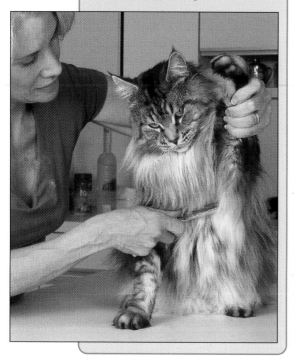

The longhaired coat of the Maine Coon is undoubtedly the essence of the breed. To neglect grooming this magnificent fur is sacrilege. If the coat is not attended to on a daily basis, it will soon look bedraggled and cause considerable discomfort to the cat. Mats will form that will prevent dead hair from being shed. These will soon enough become entangled with other debris—grass, small sticks, cat litter and even food. It is, therefore, most important that a prospective Maine Coon owner fully accepts that grooming is crucial with this breed. It should never be a chore. If done regularly, it will help bond the cat to its owner. The cat will always be a joy to behold and its owner will be very proud.

Regular grooming also enables close examination of the cat for any signs of problems. These include fleas or mites, small wounds, abrasions, swellings and bald areas. The grooming process should include inspection of the cat's ears, teeth and nails.

Always purchase the best-quality items. Avoid the use of

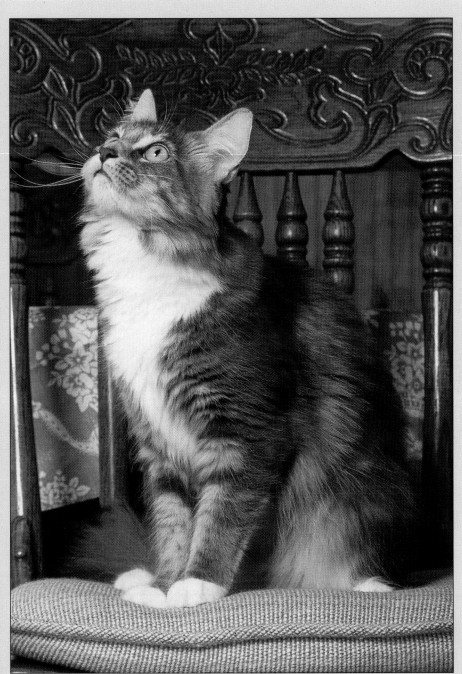

In all, Maine Coons are easy to keep, provided the owner brushes the cat regularly.

A medium-toothed metal comb helps to keep the Maine Coon's long hair untangled.

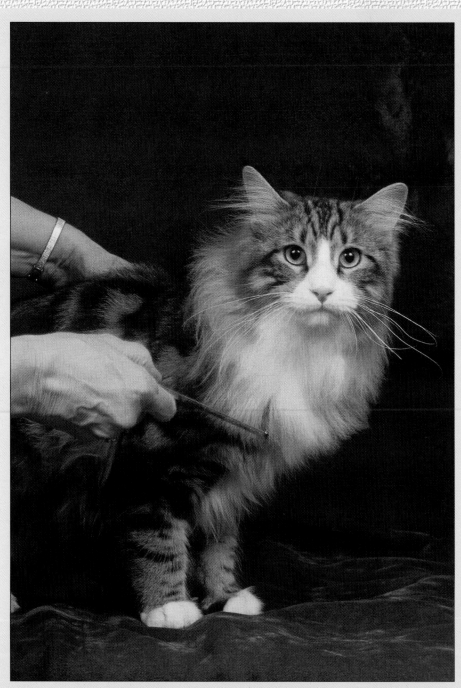

low-cost plastic-toothed combs and brushes. These create static electricity. This results in fly-away and crinkled hair that is not the best state for this breed's coat.

Before we discuss grooming procedures, a few general points should be made. If grooming is not to be reduced to a battle between cat and owner, it is essential the kitten finds this a pleasurable experience. This will not be the case if the owner is heavy-handed in his use of the brush, and more especially the comb. The tenderest parts of the cat are its underbody parts and tail. These must be groomed with this fact always in mind, doubly so if tags have formed.

Some owners groom the cat on their laps, others on tables. This author prefers a table. Ensure the surface is of a non-slip type— a rubber mat is recommended for this purpose. Again, some owners will commence with the comb, but it is better to use the brush first. It is more forgiving, thus gentle. It avoids unnecessary pulling of the hair.

## BRUSHING

Commence on the neck and brush down the fur to the tail. This will remove any small bits of detritus in the coat. Next brush down the chest, body sides and flanks. With the kitten now familiar with the feel of the brush, gently turn and secure the kitty on its back while

## GROOMING EQUIPMENT

The following will be required for complete grooming:
1. Round-ended, cushioned pin brush
2. Bristle brush
3. Medium-toothed metal comb with handle
4. Flea comb
5. A pair of guillotine nail clippers
6. Powder (If the cat is dark coloured and required for exhibition, a soft chamois leather is useful.)
7. Supply of cotton wool and cotton buds
8. Plastic pouring jug
9. Spray attachment for taps
10. Cat shampoo (Those for dogs are not suitable for felines. A baby shampoo can be used but is not as effective as one formulated for cats.)
11. One or two quality towels
12. Good hair dryer (the quieter the better)
13. Non-slip rubber mat
14. Good-sized plastic bowl with a rubber mat placed inside (to use as bath if sink is not suitable)
15. Medium-soft toothbrush and feline toothpaste (A saline solution is an alternative, but is less tasty.)
16. An appropriately sized plastic or other container in which to keep kitty's boutique apparel

## HAIRBALLS (Trichobezoar)

When cats self-groom, they invariably swallow some of their hairs. Normally these do not create a problem. However, if many dead hairs are in the coat, these may be licked and swallowed to accumulate in the stomach as hairballs. These are more common in longhaired breeds than in those with short hair. Hairballs may create intestinal blockages that may so irritate the cat's intestinal tract that it vomits the hairball or voids it via its faecal matter.

If the hairball is not removed, and the cat displays reduced appetite, veterinary assistance is needed. Regular grooming greatly reduces the risk of this condition. Additionally, a teaspoon of liquid paraffin or other laxative once a week may be helpful in cats prone to this problem. A laxative, however, is unlikely to remove an existing hairball. Pineapple juice containing the enzyme bromelain may break down small furballs. One teaspoonful a day for three days is the recommended dosage.

its belly is brushed. Groom the tail by forming a parting with the brush and grooming the fur at right angles.

This completed, brush against the lie of the fur. Commence on the neck and brush a few inches at a time, working around the body as before. As each few inches are commenced, a little baby powder can be sprinkled around the hair roots. As this is brushed and combed out, it will

## CLEAN CATS

Cats are self-groomers. They use their barbed tongues and front paws for grooming. Some cats never groom themselves, while others spend up to a third of their waking hours grooming themselves. Licking stimulates certain skin glands that make the coat waterproof.

clean the fur, remove grease, and help to keep it tag-free. Talcum powder can be used but it may cause irritation. Powdered chalk is another long-established alternative.

Finish by brushing with the lie: the hair should then be tag-free. Now combing will be easier. A tip for show-cat owners is that the use of powder in the coat is most advantageous in the lighter coat colours. Use powder sparingly in the darker ones. The chamois leather is better to polish the darker coat. It produces a better shine than if excess powder has been used.

## COMBING

Combing should be done in the same manner as the brushing, except that the final comb need not be done with the lie in most varieties. Combing against the lie is a good opportunity to see if there are any parasites present.

## RETRACTABLE CLAWS

When at rest, a cat's claws are retracted. The muscles hold the claws in their sheaths. The claw is then extended if the cat wishes to attack prey, defend itself, grab an object or climb. That is why your cat's claws are not always visible. This is true for all species of felines except the cheetah, which is unable to retract its claws, except when it is very young.

## DECLAWING

Declawing is the surgical removal of all of the claw (or nail) and the first toe joint. This practice is heavily frowned upon and even illegal in some countries, such as the United Kingdom. Unfortunately, in some areas of the world this procedure is still performed. Some owners only have the claws from the front feet removed; others do all four feet. An alternative surgical procedure is removing the tendon that allows the cat to protract its claws. This procedure, referred to as a tendonectomy, as compared to an onychectomy (removal of the claws), is less traumatic for the cat. Claws still must be filed and trimmed after a tendonectomy.

Declawing is not always 100% successful. In two-thirds of the cases the cats recovered in 72 hours. Only 4–5% of the cats hadn't recovered within a fortnight. About 3% of the cats had their claws grow back!

## DRY SHAMPOO

A dry bath may be preferred to a wet one during very cold weather or when the cat is not well enough for a water bath. Sprinkle dry shampoo into the coat and give it a good brushing. This will remove excess grease and dirt without being as thorough as a wet bath. Be very sure all the powder is brushed from the fur to avoid potential irritation and consequential scratching.

These often favour the tail base or the neck behind the ears. However, in the tabby it should be because this will best show off the pattern. If any mats should be found in the coat, these must be teased out using the index finger and thumb of both hands. Be very careful not to pull away from the skin while doing this. It will be painful and the cat will object. Never bath a cat that has even the smallest of mats in its fur. Once soaked, these will shrink into tight balls that will be much harder to tease apart.

**BATHING**
During the course of its life, there will usually be a number of occasions when any cat will need a bath, this being more so for a longhaired breed. For the show Maine Coon, this will normally be a necessity about seven days prior to a show.

Using the kitchen sink is preferable to a bath. This saves bending and allows for better control of the cat. To prevent the cat from sliding, use a rubber mat. A spray attachment is more efficient than a jug to wet and rinse the coat. The cat should have its own towels.

The choice of shampoo is important. It should ideally be formulated for cats—do not use one for dogs. This could cause problems on a cat's coat. Baby shampoos are the best alternative. Dry shampoos in powder form are available from pet shops. Alternatives would be talcum powder, powdered chalk or heated bran flakes.

The kitten should be bathed by the time it is six months of age. This will familiarise it with the process before it matures and the process degenerates into a pitched battle. Cats have no love of bathing but can come to accept it if it does not become an unpleasant ordeal.

## CAT COATS

The long primary hairs of longhaired cats can be almost three times as long as those of a shorthaired cat. The genes for length of hair are independent of the genes for colour. The original colour of cats is the mackerel or tiger-striped pattern. This pattern was inherited from the ancestors of the house cat.

Grooming should always precede bathing, as this will remove any dead hairs. The key to success lies in ensuring that no water or shampoo is allowed to enter and irritate the eyes or ears. You should be able to cope single-handedly with a kitten. However, it may be prudent to have someone else present just in case the adult proves more of a super cat than a kitten!

The water temperature should be warm, never cold or too hot. Prepare a shampoo and water solution before commencing. Have a large towel at hand. Commence by soaking the fur of the neck, then work along the back, sides, legs and tail. Pour shampoo onto the back and work this in all directions until the cat has been fully shampooed. Next, thoroughly rinse all the shampoo away. It is essential that none be left, otherwise it may cause later irritation. The use of a hair conditioner is optional. Its main drawback is that it may make the coat too greasy within days of the bath. Gently but firmly squeeze all water from the coat. The face can be cleaned using a dampened flannel.

Give the cat a brisk rubbing to remove as much liquid as possible from the coat. Now the dryer can be used. Be very careful not to hold this too close to the fur, otherwise it may burn the skin. Keep the nozzle on the move continually. While drying, it is best to be grooming the coat at the same time. This will need the help of another family member to hold the cat while you dry and groom. If the drying process is done correctly, the cat will actually enjoy this part of its grooming once familiar with it.

When the cat is dry, it should be given a final good brushing, then kept indoors for a couple of hours to ensure it is thoroughly dry. Baby powder can be used

**The Maine Coon's coat is a thing of beauty, and the owner must maintain it to show off its natural splendour.**

Cats typically groom their own claws, though some owners find it necessary to clip them short to avoid accidental scratching.

before the final brushing. The Maine Coon will now look and smell magnificent.

## EARS, EYES AND NAILS

When inspecting the ears, look for any signs of dirt. This can be gently wiped away using a dampened cotton bud or one with just a little baby or vegetable oil

### HAIR GROWTH

Cat's body hairs grow from the follicles, which are connected to the dermis. Tactile hairs (whiskers) are thicker and longer, originating three times deeper than the normal body hairs.

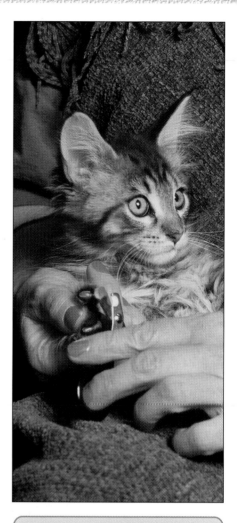

### PRESS-ON NAILS!

A stylish and fairly successful inhibitor of scratching is a plastic covering on the nails. A plastic sheath is placed over each nail and glued on with a strong, permanent adhesive. Depending upon the cat's activity, these sheaths last from one to three months.

on it. Never attempt to probe into the ear. If the ear is very waxed, this may indicate any of various health problems. A visit to the vet is recommended. The corner of the eyes can be gently wiped with damp cotton wool to remove any dust that occasionally accumulates.

Inspection of a cat's claws is achieved by firstly restraining it while on its back on your lap or held against your chest. Hold the paw and apply pressure to the top of this with your thumb. The nail will appear from its sheath. If the nail needs trimming, use the appropriate trimmers.

It is vital you do not cut into, or even too close to, the quick, which is a blood vessel. This can be seen as a darker area of the nail in pink-clawed cats. It is more difficult, or not possible, to see the quick in dark-coloured nails. In such instances, trim less. You may need a helper to do the trimming or the holding. If in doubt, let your vet do this for you. If cats have ample access to scratching posts, they will only infrequently, if ever, require their nails to be trimmed.

## TEETH

From its youngest days, your kitten should become familiar with having its teeth cleaned. Many owners do not give their cats' teeth the attention they should. This has become progressively more important due to the soft-diet regimens of modern cats. Initially, gently rub the kitten's teeth using a soft cloth on which toothpaste has been placed. This will accustom the kitten to having its teeth touched as well as to the taste of the tooth cleaner. When this is no problem for the kitten, you can progress to a soft toothbrush and ultimately one of medium hardness. Periodically, let your vet check the cat's mouth.

**These are the proud teeth of a carnivore!**

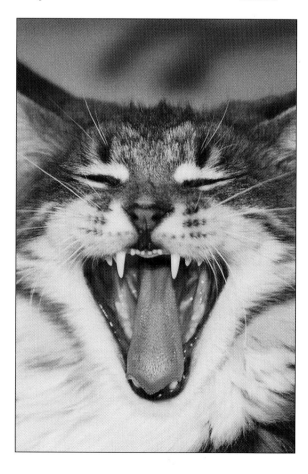

## WHY WHISKERS?

Cats are famous for their whiskers. The whiskers are tactile hairs by which cats feel. Most tactile hairs are on the cat's face, mostly on the upper lip and around the eyes, and on the wrist (carpus). These carpal hairs are extremely sensitive and are found on many predatory animals that use their front paws for holding their victims.

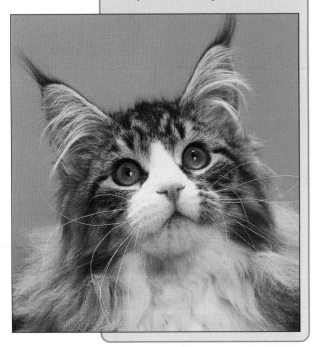

One of the outstanding virtues of cats is that they are easy to live with. They are fastidious in their personal habits related to grooming and toilet routines and basically require very little of their owners. Nonetheless, behavioural problems in cats can occur, and an owner needs to understand all the possible causes and solutions. You may never encounter a single problem with your cat, but it pays to be prepared should your feline charge disrupt your domestic bliss.

### THE BASIS OF TRAINING

The most effective means of training a cat is via reinforcement of success. A cat learning from lavish praise of doing what is required will want to repeat the action to gain more affection. There are no potential negative side effects. Conversely, when scolding or other methods of discipline are used, there is always the possibility that the cat will not relate the punishment to what the owner had intended.

For example, you cannot discipline for something done in the past. The past is anything much longer than a few minutes ago. If you call the cat to you and punish it for something done hours earlier, it cannot relate to that action. It will relate the discipline to the act of going to you when called! This will create insecurity in the pet, increasing the risk that more problems will develop.

## REMEDIAL METHODS

When faced with a problem, firstly try to pinpoint the likely cause(s). Next, consider the remedial options. Be sure these will not result in negative side effects

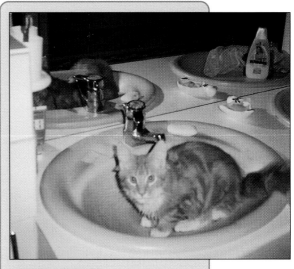

## THE TRUTH ABOUT CATS AND DOGS

Cats are unique in having the scrotum fully haired, a marked difference from their canine counterparts. This led one keen observer to say that cats were not small dogs! Dogs were domesticated well before cats since cats only served to protect the abode of the owner from rodents, while dogs served as guards, hunters, herders, exterminators and as loyal companions that were readily trainable. Cats have always been more independent and less trainable.

## SETTING THE GROUND RULES

From the outset you must determine the ground rules and stick to them. Always remember that your companion's patterns of behaviour begin to form from the moment it first arrives at your home. If the future adult is not to be given outdoor freedom, then do not let it outdoors as a kitten. If any rooms are to be out of bounds to the adult, then do not let the kitten into them. Stability is vital in a cat's life; without it, the result will be stress and its related behavioural changes.

Ground rules of how to handle the kitten and to respect its privacy when sleeping should be instilled into all children. The cat's meals should be given at about the same time each day. This will have the secondary advantage that the pet's toilet habits will be more predictable.

## CAUSES OF LITTER-BOX PROBLEMS

1. The litter tray is dirty. Cats never like to use a previously fouled tray.
2. The litter has been changed to one of a different texture that the cat does not like. Generally the finer-grained litters are the most favoured.
3. A scented litter is being used to mask odours. The cat may not like the scent. Such litters should not be necessary if the tray is regularly cleaned.
4. The tray is regularly cleaned, but an ammonium or pine-based disinfectant is being used. This may aggravate the cat's sensitive nasal mucous membranes. Additionally, the phenols in pine are dangerous to cats.
5. The litter tray is located too close to the cat's food and water bowls. Cats do not like to eat near litter trays or to defecate/urinate close to their feeding areas.
6. Another cat or free-roaming pet has been added to the household and is causing the cat stress. In multi-cat households, two or more trays may be needed.
7. There is insufficient litter in the tray. There should be about 2 inches of litter depth.
8. The cat has developed a fear of using the tray due to an upsetting experience. For instance, the owner may have caught the cat as it finished using the tray in order that it could be given a medicine. Children may be disturbing it while it is relieving itself.
9. The cat is ill (or elderly) and is unable to control its bowel movements. Veterinary attention is required.
10. The cat, because of one or more of the previous problems, has established other more favourable areas.

linked to you. Always be the paragon of patience. Some problems may be extremely complex and deeply rooted within the cat's behaviour patterns. As such, they are habits not easily changed, and often difficult to analyse. In discussing the following problems it is hoped you will understand the basic ways in which to correct other unwanted patterns of behaviour that might occur. But always remember it is far better to avoid a problem than to correct it.

## THE LITTER TRAY

A very common problem for some owners is that their cat starts to attend to its toileting needs anywhere other than in its litter tray. The problem may become apparent from the time the kitten gets to its new home, or it may develop at any time during its life. So, let us start from the beginning and try to avoid the situation.

Until you are satisfied that the kitten is using its litter tray consistently, do not give it access to carpeted rooms. The youngster should already have been litter-trained well before you obtained it. You should obtain a litter tray similar to the one it is already familiar with. It is also important that the same brand of litter is used, at least initially. Place the tray in a quiet spot so the kitten has privacy when attending to its needs.

A kitten will need to relieve itself shortly after it has eaten, exercised or been sleeping. Watch it carefully at these times. If it stoops to attend to its needs other than in the litter tray, calmly lift it into its tray and scratch at the litter. Never shout or panic the kitty by making a sudden rush for it. If it does what is hoped, give it lots of praise. If it steps out of the tray, gently place it back in for a few seconds.

If nothing happens, be patient and wait, then repeat the process. If it fouls the floor when you are not watching, simply clean this up and wait for the next opportunity to transport the kitten to its tray. It rarely takes long for a kitten to consistently use this. Be very sure the tray is kept spotless. Cats have no more desire to use a fouled toilet than you do. Every few days, give the cat tray a good wash. Use soapy water and always rinse it thoroughly. Allow it to dry, then fill the tray with litter to depth of about 1.5–2 inches.

By identifying the cause(s) of litter-box problems, the correction is often self-evident. However, once the cause has been corrected, this is only part of the solution. Next, the habit of fouling other places must be overcome. Where possible, do not let the cat enter rooms in which it has started to foul until the odour has had time to fully disperse. Wash the area of the fouling then treat carpets and soft

## MAN MEETS CAT

Early man, perhaps 8000 years ago, started his symbiotic relationship with domestic cats, *Felis catus* or *Felis domesticus*. The cats killed and ate the rats and mice and probably anything else which crawled and was small, which early man attracted and considered as pests. Early man reciprocated by allowing the cat to sleep in his cave, hut or tent. Cats, being essentially nocturnal, kept the small mammals (rats, mice, etc.) from disturbing the sleep of early man.

As early man evolved to modern man, the domestic cat came along as an aid to pest control. This was especially true of peoples who farmed, as farmers were plagued with rodents. Though most cats were not selectively bred for their predatory skills, it was obvious that those cats that were the best hunters were more successful in evolutionary terms than the cats that were more meek. Modern cats have changed very little from the cats from which they descended. There are still, today, cats that are very predatory, attacking small mammals and birds; there are also meek cats which, unless fed by their owners, would perish in a competitive cat society.

It has been shown repeatedly that if kittens are socialised in a proper manner, they will become peaceful pets. This includes lions and tigers. If the kittens are not socialised properly, they revert immediately to their aggressive, predatory behaviours.

If your Maine
Coon is the
only cat in
your home,
has been
altered and is
not given
access to the
outdoors, you
will most
likely not have
a problem
with scent
marking.

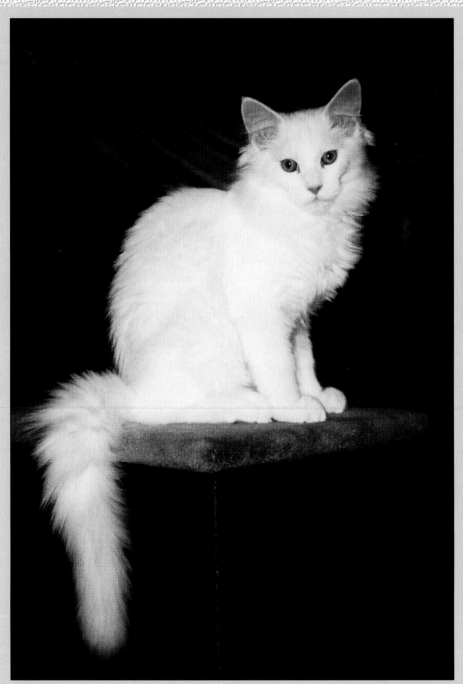

furnishings with an odour neutraliser (not an air freshener) from your pet shop or vet.

If the cat cannot be prevented from entering certain rooms, then cover previously fouled areas with plastic sheeting or tinfoil, or rinse the area with white vinegar. Also, place a litter tray in the fouled room while the retraining is underway. It may help if a different size, type or colour of tray is used.

## SCENT MARKING

Both sexes scent mark, though males are more prolific. It is a means of advertising their presence in a territory, thus an integral part of their natural behaviour. Spraying is usually done against a vertical surface. It tells other males that the individual is residing in that territory. Alternatively, it will tell a female that a male lives close by— or it will tell the male that a female is in the area. It is thus a very important part of a cat's social language.

Neutered cats have little need to mark their territory, or leave their 'calling card' to attract mates. They are far less likely to spray than those not altered. However, scent marking may commence when the cat is attempting to assert its position in the household.

To overcome the problem of scent marking, the first need is to try to identify if there is an obvious specific cause. In multi-cat households, it also requires positive identification of the sprayer(s) and the favoured spraying surface. Try giving the cat more freedom and its own sleeping place, if it does not have one.

## CAUSES OF SCENT MARKING

1. Another cat, or pet, has been introduced to the household. It may be bullying the resident cat. This problem may resolve itself when the two get to know each other. The more cats there are, the longer it may take for the situation to be resolved. Much will depend on the space within which the cats may roam and whether they are able to avoid those they dislike.
2. The birth of a new family member may annoy the cat for a while, especially if its owner suddenly gives it less attention.
3. A friend staying in the home for a few days may not like cats. If 'shooed' away a number of times, the cat may feel it should assert its position and mark it.
4. If the cat is given outdoor freedom, a bully may have moved into the territory. Having lost control of its own garden, the pet may assert its territorial boundaries within its home. If a cat flap is used, another cat may be entering the home and this will trigger the resident to scent mark.

Covering the sprayed surface with plastic sheeting, or a cloth impregnated with a scent the cat does not like (such as lemon, pepper or bleach), may be successful. Spraying the cat with a water pistol when catching it in the action is a common ploy. Veterinary treatment with the hormone progesterone may prove effective—discuss this with your vet.

## SCRATCHING

Scratching is a normal feline characteristic. Unfortunately, house

### SCRATCHING FURNITURE

All cats need to scratch in order to maintain their claws in good condition. For this reason, one or more scratching posts strategically placed in the cat's most-used rooms will normally prevent the problem. Place the post in front of the scratched furniture. It can be moved steadily further away once the furniture is ignored. This is a problem that may become more manifest when cats are not allowed outdoors and have insufficient indoor provisions to scratch.

### CAT SCRATCH DISEASE

An objectionable habit of many poorly raised kittens is their exuberant jumping to greet you. This flying jump may result in the kitten's being attached to your body; otherwise it will fall to the floor and may injure itself. In the attachment process, your skin will usually be pierced, and this is a health concern. All cat scratches and bites should be thoroughly cleaned with an antiseptic soap. If a sore appears at the site of the wound, you should visit your family doctor immediately.

Cat scratch disease is a well-known problem. It is caused by a bacterium (*Rochalimaea henselae*) that is usually easily treated with antibiotics. However, more and more cases show resistance to the usual antibiotics.

Untreated cat scratch fever may result in an enlargement of the lymph nodes, imitating a cancerous condition known as lymphoma. Interestingly enough, the lymph nodes, upon biopsy, may show large Reid-Sternberg cells, which are a characteristic of Hodgkins lymphoma. The bottom line is that cat scratches should be taken seriously.

cats tend to destroy furniture to satisfy their need to scratch. Feral or outdoor cats usually attack a tree because trees are readily accessible and the bark of the tree suits their needs perfectly. If the outdoor cat lives in a pride, it will scratch more than a solitary feral cat. The reasons for this are known. When

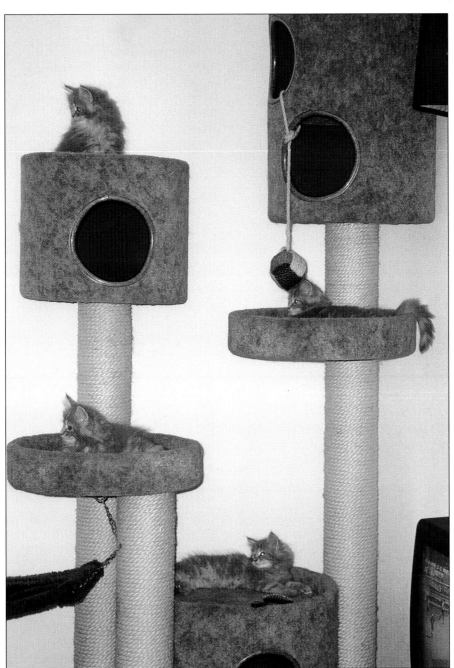

Scratching is a normal feline activity. To avoid damage to your furniture and carpets, you should supply a suitable outlet for your cat's scratching needs.

## FERAL CATS

Feral cats are, as a general rule, undernourished. They spend most of their time searching for food. Consequently, those feral cats that have kittens spend less time with their kittens than do well-nourished cats. It has been shown that kittens born to feral mothers are usually unsocial and show little affection for their mothers. Obviously, they would show a similar lack of affection for a human. That's one of the reasons that feral kittens make poor pets and should neither be adopted nor brought into your home. Kittens, which for any reason are separated from their mothers at the age of two weeks, develop an attitude of fear and wariness. They escape from contact with other cats or humans and can even be dangerous if they feel trapped.

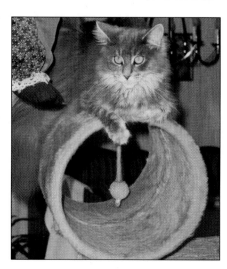

This type of scratching post, with a hanging toy inside, will satisfy two of the cat's desires—to scratch and to play.

cats scratch, they leave tell-tale marks. Parts of the nail's sheath exudate from glands located between their claws, and the visual aspects are the marks which cats leave to impress or advertise their presence.

Cat owners whose cats scratch should not consider the scratching as an aggressive behavioural disorder. It is normal for cats to scratch. Keeping your cat's claws clipped or filed so they are as short as possible, without causing bleeding, may inhibit scratching. Your vet can teach you how to do this. Clipping and filing should be started when the kitten is very young. Starting this when the cat has matured is much more difficult and may even be dangerous.

There are ways to control annoying cat scratching. Certainly, the easiest way is to present your cat with an acceptable cat scratching post. These are usually available at most local pet shops. The post should be covered with a material that is to your cat's liking. If your cat has already indicated what it likes to scratch, it usually is a good idea to cover the post with this same material. Veterinary surgeons often suggest that you use sandpaper, as this will reduce the cat's nails quickly and it will not have the urge to scratch. Certainly using hemp, carpeting, cotton towelling or bark is worth a try. Once the cat uses the post, it usually will have neither a desire nor a need to scratch any place else.

Besides the physical need to scratch, many cats have a psychological need to scratch. This is evidenced by where they scratch versus what they scratch. Often cats prefer semi-darkness. Some prefer flat surfaces and not vertical surfaces. Some prefer public areas in which their human friends are present instead of secluded areas. It may be stress related, as with scent marking, because scratching is another territorial-marking behaviour. In any case, the idea is to get your cat to scratch the post and not the carpets, furniture, drapes or the duvet on your bed.

Introduce your cat to the post by rubbing its paws on the post, hoping it will take the hint. Oftentimes the cat voluntarily attacks the post. Unfortunately, oftentimes it doesn't. If you catch your cat scratching in a forbidden area, startle it with a loud shout, by banging a folded newspaper against your hand or with something else which will take its attention away from scratching. Never hit the cat. This will only get a revengeful reaction that might be dangerous.

## RUBBISH RUMMAGING

Cats are inquisitive and may decide to have a good look through any interesting rubbish bins that are exuding an enticing odour. Normally, the answer is to remove the bin. However, if the attraction

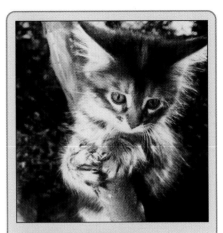

### TIDY TOILETING
During the kitten's stay in the nest box, the mother will assist or even stimulate bowel and urine elimination, at least for the first month of the kitten's life. The mother also does the clean-up work in the nest box. But once the kitten is older, it becomes capable of relieving itself out of the nest box. Usually the kitten likes sand, soft earth or something that seems absorbent and is easily moved with its paws. By the time the kitten is two months old, it should develop the discipline of covering its elimination. Not all kittens develop this discipline, though the use of an absorbent clay litter seems to be helpful in developing this discipline in young cats. Your local pet shop will have various cat litters to offer you.

always seems to be kitchen rubbish, there may be a nutritional problem. It may be searching for food because it is being underfed! It may alternatively be receiving an

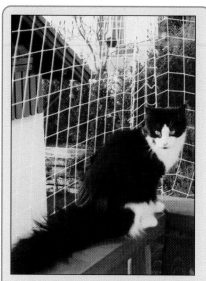

## CATS AND OTHER PETS

If you already have a pet cat or cats, or dogs, or almost any other animal that isn't small, creeping or crawling, your cat can usually be socialised so the other pet and the cat will tolerate each other. In many cases, cats and dogs become quite friendly and attached to each other, often making frequent physical contacts, sleeping together or even sharing each other's food.

## MARKING TERRITORY

Cats are geographical by nature and they mark their territories in the usual way...by spraying their urine. The frequency of spraying is amazing! A non-breeding male cat that is not within its own turf will spray about 13 times an hour while travelling through the new territory. A breeding male will spray almost twice as much. One reports states that free-ranging males spray 62.6 times an hour—that's more than once a minute!

Cat urine is recognisable for at least 24 hours and male cats spend a lot of time sniffing the area. Females spend less time, but both sexes easily recognise the urine from male cats that are strange to the area.

unbalanced diet and is trying to satisfy its inner need for a given missing ingredient.

Another possibility, and one which may be more appropriate to the indoors-only cat, is boredom or loneliness. These conditions can only be remedied by greater interaction between owner and cat and/or obtaining a companion feline.

Clearly the cause should be identified. The immediate solution is to place the rubbish in a cupboard or similar place that is out of the cat's reach. This type of solution is called removal of the re-enforcer. It is a common method of overcoming problems across a number of unwanted behaviours. However, it does not correct the underlying problem that must still be addressed.

The first-time cat owner should not think that the problems discussed will likely be encoun-tered. They are only met when the cat's environment is lacking in some way. Always remember that the older cat may have problems with bowel control. An extra litter tray at another location in the home will usually remedy this situation. Finally, if a problem is found and you are not able to remedy it, do seek the advice of your vet or breeder.

There are many kinds of litter trays and even more kinds of litter. Litters vary by scent and absorption characteristics and vary greatly in price. Some of the more expensive brands outlast the others, making them a better-smelling, afford-able choice.

## CAVEAT EMPTOR

When purchasing a kitten for breeding, make certain that the seller knows what your intentions are. If a kitten is registered on the non-active register, this means it was not considered by its breeder to be good enough for breeding. Any kittens bred from such a cat cannot be registered. You should also check that the mother of the kitten/young adult you are interested in has tested negative for feline leukaemia and that all other vaccinations are current.

While the idea of becoming a breeder may appeal to many owners, the reality is more difficult than is often appreciated. It requires dedication, considerable investment of time and money, and the ability to cope with many heart-wrenching decisions and failures.

It would be quite impossible to discuss the complexities of practical breeding in only one chapter, so we will consider the important requirements of being a breeder plus basic feline reproductive information. This will enable you to better determine if, indeed, this aspect of the hobby is for you.

### BEING A BREEDER

Apart from great affection for the breed, a successful breeding programme requires quantifiable objectives. Foremost among these is the rearing of healthy kittens free from known diseases. Next is the desire to produce offspring that are as good as, indeed better than, their parents.

Such objectives ensure that a breeder will endeavour to

maintain standards and reduce or remove from the cat population any instances of dangerous diseases and conditions. Only stock registered and tested free of major diseases should ever be used. Adopting such a policy helps to counteract those who breed from inferior and often unhealthy cats.

To be a successful breeder, you will need to become involved in the competition side of the hobby. Only via this route will you be able to determine if your programme is successful or not. Always remember that even the top-winning breeders still produce quite a high percentage of kittens that will only be of pet quality. There will be many disappointments along the road to even modest success.

## THE DISADVANTAGES OF BREEDING

There are many rewards to be gained from breeding, but the disadvantages should also be carefully considered. Kittens are demanding, especially once they are over three weeks of age. Rearing, vaccination, registration and veterinary bills will be costly. Any thoughts of profit should be dispelled. Homes must be found for the kittens which will entail receiving many telephone calls— some at very inconvenient hours.

Many potential buyers will prove to be either unsuitable or

## TOO MANY CATS

There are already too many cats in the world. In many countries, thousands of pathetic-looking felines can be seen wandering the streets in a badly emaciated state. They live tormented lives and have become a major social problem in many areas. There can be no excuse for these feral populations in developed Western nations. Quite frankly, some people who own cats, including some pedigreed owners, lack a sense of responsibility.

Cats allowed to roam in a non-neutered state are by far the main reason for the overpopulation problem. Unless a cat is of show or breeding quality, there is not a single justification for it to be bred or to remain in a non-neutered state. If your cat was purchased as a pet, you should help to resolve this global problem by having it neutered at the earliest possible date. This will make it a far healthier, happier and less problematic pet.

## TOM FOOLERY

A non-neutered male cat kept as a single pet has little or no value for breeding purposes. It must be exhibited so it can gain some fame. The owner must have modern facilities to house both males and females. Females are always serviced at the home of the stud owner. This is extra responsibility and cost.

Such a male cannot be given any freedom to roam. If the tom is kept indoors, its scent-marking odours will often become intolerable. Even kept outdoors in a suitable cat pen, it will spray regularly to attract the attention of any females in the area. Toms are more assertive and often more aggressive than neutered males.

If they are allowed any outdoor freedom, they will become involved in battles with the local toms. Consequently, they will soon lose their handsome looks! Most cat breeders do not even keep males because of the problems and costs they entail. These cats are best kept in catteries where the owners have the time, the funds and everything else needed to justify their retention.

## CAT CALLS

Females left in a non-spayed state are far more at risk from diseases and infections of the uterus. When in heat, the female becomes unusually affectionate and provocative. Her calls, a sound once heard never forgotten, can become extremely annoying if she is left unmated.

'time-wasters' looking for the cheapest pedigreed cat obtainable. Kittens may die, while cats of any age could test positive for a major disease. They may have to be put to sleep or given to a caring person who understands the problem.

Owning a number of cats will mean investing in cat pens. When females come into heat, they will try to escape and mate with any local tom with a twinkle in his eye! Their scent and calls will attract roving Romeos who will gather near your home and involve themselves in a series of raucous battles. Holidays and matings will need to be planned around hoped-for litter dates. All in all, owning only one or two breeding females is a major commitment.

## THE BREEDING QUEEN

A female used for breeding purposes is called a queen. The principal requirement of such a cat is that she is an excellent example of the breed. This does not mean she must be a show winner. Many a winning exhibition cat has proved to have little breeding value. This is because a show cat gains success purely on its appearance; however, it may not pass those looks to its offspring.

A good breeding female may lack that extra something needed to be a top winner. Yet, she may pass on most of her excellent features to her offspring. Much will depend on the breeding line from which she was produced. Therefore, any potential breeder must research existing breeders to ascertain which have good track records of producing consistently high-quality cats. In truth, and sadly, few newcomers in their haste to become breeders make this extra effort. This can result in becoming disillusioned if the female produces only average to inferior kittens.

## ROAMING ROMEOS

Males cats, toms, have extended testicles very early in life. By about nine months of age, the tom is capable of mating with a queen. Both queens and toms are polygamous, and it is not uncommon for a queen to have a litter containing kittens fathered by different toms.

## THE MALE STUD

The selection of a suitable stud should have been planned months before, as it can take some time to find the best male to use. It is preferred that the breeding lines of the stud are compatible with those of the female, meaning both pedigrees will carry a number of the same individuals in them. This is termed line-breeding. The ideal male will excel in those features that are considered weak in the female. You may read in other books that if a female is weak in a given feature, the ideal stud will be the total opposite. However, this can be misleading.

If the female has an overly long tail, what you do not need is a stud with a short tail. Rather, his tail should be as near the ideal length as possible. Genetically, this will improve tail length in your line without introducing unwanted genetic variance in your stock. Compensatory matings, such as short tail to long tail, will create such a variance. Once a male has been selected, ensure all his papers and vaccinations are in order. The female will be taken to the stud and left with him for a few days.

Before deciding whether breeding really is something you want to do, what would make good sense would be to neuter the pet and then become an exhibitor. When you have exhibited a number of times, your knowledge of cats will be greater, as will your contacts. You will be more aware of what quality is all about and what it will cost for a well-bred female. It will be like an apprenticeship. Whether you then become a breeder, remain an exhibitor or prefer life as a pet owner, you will be glad you heeded the words of advice given here.

## STOCK SELECTION

Stock selection revolves around health, quality, sex and age. Before these are discussed, it should be stated that many beginners unwisely rush this process. It is essential that ample time be devoted to researching from whom to purchase. This decision will influence a novice breeder's entire future endeavours.

### HEALTH

Cats should only be obtained from a breeder whose stock has been tested negative for FeLV, FIP and FIV. The stock should be current on all vaccinations and worm treatments. Additionally, its blood type should be known so as to avoid incompatibility problems.

## QUALITY

This must come in two forms. One is in the individual cat's appearance; the other is in its genetic ability to pass on the quality of its parents. The best way of obtaining these paired needs is to obtain initial stock from a breeder having a proven record of success in Maine Coons, and with the colour you plan to start with. Being well acquainted with the breed's standard will be advantageous when seeking foundation stock. A female show cat attains her titles based on her appearance, but she may not pass on those looks to her offspring. Another cat that is very sound may pass on most of her good points and thus be more valuable for breeding. Of course, all litters will be influenced by the quality of the tom used. He will account for 50% of the offspring's genes. When viewing a litter of kittens, never forget that they are the result of the genes of two cats.

## SEX

The beginner should only obtain females. The best advice is to commence with just one very sound female. By the time you have exhibited her and gained more knowledge about the finer points of the breed, you will be far better able to judge what true quality is all about. By then, you will also have made many contacts on the show circuit.

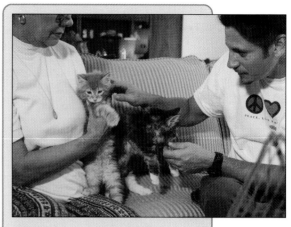

## WHAT'S A PEDIGREE WORTH?

When choosing breeding stock, never be dazzled by a pedigree. No matter how illustrious this is, it is only ever as good as the cat that bears it. If the cat is mediocre, then its prestigious pedigree is worthless from a breeding perspective. There are many other pitfalls for the novice when judging the value of a breeding line. These you must research in larger, more specialised books.

Alternatively, you may decide breeding is not for you and will have invested the minimum of time and money. A male is not needed until a breeder has become established. Even then, owning one is not essential to success. There is no shortage of quality studs. Males create many problems the novice can do without. Once experience is gained is the time to decide if owning a male would be of any particular benefit.

### AGE

There is no specific age at which stock should be purchased, but the following are suggested:

1. Most people purchase young kittens so they can enjoy them. However, with such youngsters, their ultimate quality is harder to assess.
2. Chances are improved if a kitten has already won awards in shows. This will be when she is 14 weeks to 9 months of age, but she will be more costly.
3. A quality young female that has already produced offspring is a prudent choice but will be the most expensive option.

## THE BREEDING PROCESS

Sexual maturity in cats may come as early as four months of age. Breeding should not be considered until the female is at least 12 months old, especially in the slow-maturing breeds such as those of Persian and European stock ancestry. A young cat barely out of her kitten stage may not have the required physical or psychological stability to produce and raise a vigorous litter. After her first heat, a female will normally come into heat again every two to three weeks and continue to do so until mated. The actual oestrous period lasts three to eight days. It is during this time that she is receptive to a male.

Once the mating has been

Maine Coons that are purchased for the purpose of breeding should be exhibited and evaluated before deciding to breed.

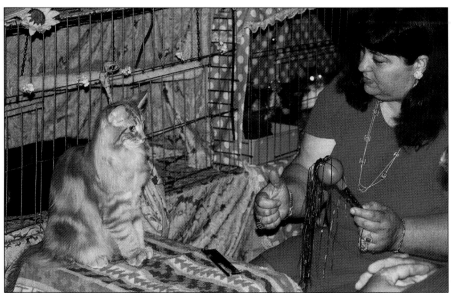

## THE HEAT IS ON

Most female cats reach sexual maturity by the time they are 28 weeks old. Females normally accept males from late winter to early fall, about a six-month period. They have a reproductive cycle of about two weeks and are in heat for about one of the two weeks. Intercourse causes the female to ovulate and pregnancy may last for about 64 days, perhaps longer in cold climates and shorter in the tropics.

successful, the time between fertilisation and birth of the young, known as the gestation period, is in the range of 59 to 67 days, 63 or 64 days being typical. The litter size will generally be two to five. Kittens are born blind and helpless, but develop rapidly. Their eyes open at about the seventh day. By 21 days they start exploring. At this time they will also be sampling solid foods. By eight weeks they can be vaccinated and neutered if required. Weaning normally commences by the age of six weeks and is completed within

two to three weeks. Kittens can go to new homes when 12 weeks old, though 14 to 16 weeks is preferred.

During this period you must decide if you wish to register the kittens or merely 'declare' them. This allows them to be registered at a later time. Obtain the necessary information and forms from your cat-registration authority. You should also consider the benefits of registering your own breeder prefix. This, however, is only worthwhile if you intend to breed on a more than casual basis. If you have decided that certain kittens are unsuitable for showing/breeding, do consider early neutering.

## NEWBORN KITTENS

Most kittens are born with body hair. Their ears and eyes, however, remain closed for about two weeks, though some ears and eyes become functional after 72 hours. Kittens should be allowed to nurse for seven weeks, longer if they will not readily eat and drink from a plate. If allowed to nurse, most kittens will stay on their mother's milk for two months or more.

## EXAMPLES OF CLASSES AT SHOWS

| | |
|---|---|
| **Open** | Any cat of the specified breed. |
| **Novice** | Cats that have never won a first prize. |
| **Limit** | Cats that have not won more than first prizes. |
| **Junior** | Cats over nine months of age but less than two years on the day of the show. |
| **Senior** | Cats over two years old. |
| **Visitors** | Cats living a given distance away from the show venue. |
| **Assessment** | Experimental breeds, which have an approved standard. |
| **Aristocrat** | Cats with one or two Challenge Certificates (or Premiers for neuters) so are not yet full Champions/Premiers. |

Without shows, the cat fancy could not exist. There would be only a handful of breeds as compared with today's ever-growing list. There would be fewer colour patterns and far less cat awareness. Given the great importance of shows to the cat fancy, it is perhaps a little surprising, and disappointing, that the majority of cat owners have never visited a feline exhibition.

Shows such as the National and the Supreme of Britain, or their equivalents in other countries, are the shop windows of the world of domestic cats. They are meeting places where breeders from all over the country compete to establish how well their breeding programmes are developing. A show is also a major social event on the cat calendar.

Whether a potential pet owner or breeder of the future, you should visit one or two shows. It is a great day out for the whole family. Apart from the wonderful selection of breeds, there are also many trade stands. If a product is available, it will be seen at the large exhibitions.

Many of the national clubs and magazines have stands. The two major shows mentioned are held in the winter months, usually November and December. However, there are hundreds of other shows staged during the year in various parts of the country. They range from small local club events to major championship breed shows and are usually advertised in the cat magazines. Your ruling cat association can also supply a list of shows.

## SHOW ORGANISATION

So you will have some idea of how things are organised, the following information will be helpful. You will learn even more by purchasing the show catalogue. This contains the names and addresses of the exhibitors and details of their cats. It also lists the prizes, indicates the show regulations and carries many interesting advertisements.

A major show revolves around three broad categories of cats:

1. Unaltered cats, meaning those that are capable of breeding.
2. Neuters.
3. Non-pedigreed cats.

There is, thus, the opportunity for every type of cat, from

### ON THE CONTINENT AND BEYOND...

In Britain the title of UK Grand Champion or Premier is won in competition with other Grand titleholders. In mainland Europe cats can become International Champions. More British cats are expected to become International Champions with the recent introduction of passports for cats, allowing cats to compete more freely on the Continent and beyond. In countries other than Britain, the way in which shows are organised and titles achieved do differ somewhat. However, they broadly follow the outline discussed here.

the best Maine Coon to the everyday 'moggie' pets, to take part. These three broad categories are divided into various sections. For example, the unaltered and neuters are divided into their respective sections, such as Longhair, Semi-Longhair, British, Foreign, Siamese and so on.

There are many more classes other than those mentioned. These include club classes and those for kittens and non-pedigreed cats.

## JUDGING

There are two ways that cats can be judged. One is pen judging, the other is bench or ring judging. In Britain, pen judging is the normal method, though bench judging is used for Best in Show. In pen judging, the judge moves around the cat pens. The cat gaining the most points when compared to the standard wins. In bench judging, stewards take the cats to the judge.

If a cat wins its class, it then competes against other class winners. By this process of elimination, a cat may go on to win the Best of Breed award. It then competes against other breed winners for the Best in Group award. The group winners compete for the Best in Show award.

A breeder can gather a number of awards during the course of a show. Even those who do not own the very best cats can take pride in gaining second, third, fourth and recommended, especially if won

at the larger shows. By progression, the top cat at a show will win its class, its breed, its section, and ultimately become the Best in Show exhibit. The titles a cat can win commence with that of Champion, or Premier in the case of neuters. A Grand Champion is made after winning in competition with others of its same status. The same applies to a Grand Premier. The judging system may vary from one country to another, but the basis remains as outlined.

## THE SHOW CAT

When a cat is seen preening in its pen, the hard work that has gone into its preparation is rarely appreciated. Exhibits must be in peak condition and their coats in full bloom. The potential exhibit must be gradually trained to spend hours in its show pen. It must display no fear or aggression towards strangers, such as the stewards or the judges. These must be able to physically examine it, including its ears and teeth; it also involves being lifted into the air. If a cat scratches or bites a judge, or any other show official, it is automatically withdrawn from the show. A repeat of this in the future would result, in most instances, in the cat's show career being terminated by the

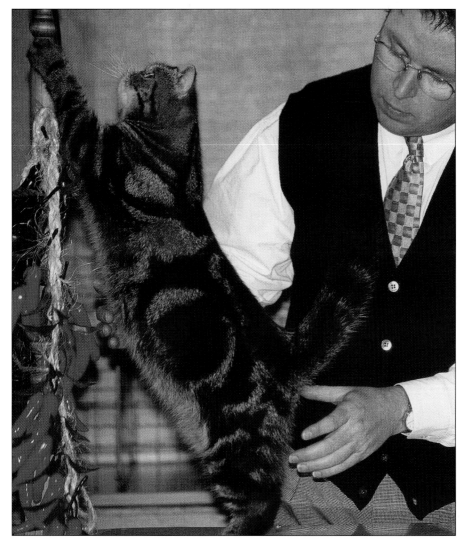

**Even if you do not intend to show your cat, a visit to a cat show can be very informative. The show cat must be in peak condition and its coat in full bloom.**

ruling association.

Apart from being comfortable with people peering into its pen, the cat must be able to endure long journeys to the show venue. Unless properly trained, the cat may become a nervous, aggressive feline that will have a very short show career.

Obviously the cat must display quality. This means having none of the major faults that would prevent it from

## CLASSES FOR NON-PEDIGREED CATS

For non-pedigreed cats there are many classes, which include those for single colours, bicolours, tabbies, half-pedigreed and so on. In this section are many delightful classes, such as those for cats owned by senior citizens, by young children (by age group), best original stray or rescued cat, best personality, most unusual looking, most photogenic and best older cat. Within this cat section can be seen some truly gorgeous felines. There is no doubt that the pet classes have been the springboard that has launched many a top breeder into the world of pedigreed cats.

## BECOMING AN EXHIBITOR

Before any hobbyist enters a show, he is advised to join a local cat club. Here, hobbyists will meet local breeders who will not only assess their cats for them but also provide help on many other topics. The novice exhibitor could attend one or two shows with an exhibitor in order to learn the ropes. During this period, he can become familiar with the show rules and regulations. These are quite extensive, intended to safeguard the best interests of the hobby, the exhibitors and, most importantly, the cats.

It is of interest to note that some breeders own cats in partnership with other fanciers. This is useful when one person enjoys the breeding and the other the exhibition side. It enables both to really be involved in the hobby to a level that might not have been possible for either on his own. So, whether you fancy being an exhibitor or just love cats, do make a point of visiting the next major show in your area.

gaining a first prize. These are listed in the breed standard. The meaning of quality is very flexible. You do not need to own a potential champion to be a successful exhibitor. The cat must also be registered with the association under whose rules the show is being run. In Britain, this will be the Governing Council of the Cat Fancy (GCCF) or The Cat Association of Britain.

As in anything competitive, exhibits can gain prizes at the lower levels of a hobby without having any realistic chance of awards in the major shows. Owning such exhibits is often part of a top breeder/exhibitor's portfolio from their early days in the hobby. Others may never move beyond the smaller shows but still gain reputations for owning sound stock. They thoroughly enjoy being involved at their given level.

If the idea of exhibiting appeals to you, the best way to make a start is to join a local club. There you will not only be advised on all procedures, but will assuredly make many new friends. Exhibiting can be costly in cash and time, but you can focus on the more local shows while attending the larger ones as a visitor.

Your Maine Coon must be properly socialised to succeed at a cat show. The judges engage in 'hands-on' inspection of the cat, handling that the cat must accept without fuss.

Maintaining a cat in the peak of good health revolves around the implementation of a sound husbandry strategy. At the basic level, this means being responsible about feeding, cleanliness and grooming.

### A LONG, HEALTHY LIFE
As veterinary surgeons make medical advances in the health care of cats, the longevity of the typical house cat is improving. Certainly ages between 15 and 18 years are not uncommon, and reports of cats living more than 20 years are predictable.

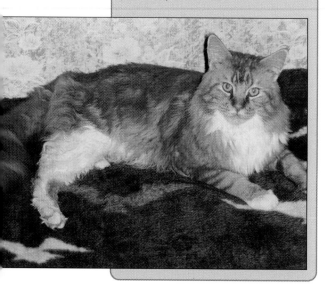

However, in spite of an owner's best efforts in these matters, cats may still become ill due to other causes. Although owners can attempt to prevent, identify and react to problems, only a vet is qualified to diagnose and advise and/or effect remedies. Attempts by owners or 'informed' friends to diagnose and treat for specific diseases are dangerous and potentially life-threatening to the cat.

### SELECTING A VETERINARY SURGEON
Your selection of a veterinary surgeon should not be based upon personality (as most are) but upon convenience to your home. You want a vet who is close because you might have emergencies or need to make multiple visits for treatments. You want a vet who has services that you might require such as nail clipping and bathing, as well as sophisticated pet supplies and a good reputation for ability and responsiveness. There is nothing more frustrating than having to wait a day or more to get a response from your veterinary surgeon.

All veterinary surgeons are licensed and their diplomas and/or certificates should be displayed in their waiting rooms. There are, however, many veterinary specialities that usually require further studies and internships. There are specialists in heart problems (veterinary cardiologists), skin problems (veterinary dermatologists), teeth and gum problems (veterinary dentists), eye problems (veterinary ophthalmologists) and x-rays (veterinary radiologists), as well as vets who have specialities in reproduction, nutrition and behaviour. Most veterinary surgeons do routine surgery, such as neutering and stitching up wounds. When the problem affecting your cat is serious, it is not unusual or impudent to get another medical opinion, although in Britain you are obliged to advise the vets concerned about this. You might also want to compare costs among several veterinary surgeons. Sophisticated health care and veterinary services can be very costly. It is not infrequent that important decisions are based upon financial considerations.

## PREVENTATIVE MEDICINE

It is much easier, less costly and more effective to practise preventative medicine than to fight bouts of illness and disease. Properly bred kittens come from

## KEEPING YOUR CAT HEALTHY

Although there are a multitude of ailments, diseases and accidents that could befall a cat, all but the most minor of problems can be avoided with good management. The following tips are a recipe for keeping your cat in the peak of health.

- Make sure it is vaccinated and in other ways protected from each of the major diseases. It must also receive annual boosters to maintain immunity.
- Have periodic checks made by your vet to see if your cat has worms.
- Ensure the cat receives an adequate diet that is both appealing and balanced.
- Have the kitten neutered if it is not to be used for breeding.
- Ensure the cat's litter tray, food/water vessels and grooming tools are always maintained in spotless condition.
- Do not let your cat out overnight or when you are away working or shopping.
- Always wash your hands after gardening or petting other people's pets.
- Groom your cat daily. If this is done, you will more readily notice fleas or other problems than if grooming was done less frequently.
- Never try to diagnose and treat problems that are clearly of an internal type. Remember, even the most informed of breeders is not a vet and unable to reliably diagnose problems for you or advise treatments. Contact your vet.
- If you are ever in doubt about the health of your cat, do not delay in discussing your concerns with your vet. Delays merely allow problems to become more established.

> ## A DELICATE HEART
> A cat's heart is as delicate as a human's heart, but it is much smaller. At full maturity, the queen's heart weighs between 9–12 grammes. The tom's heart is heavier, weighing 11–18 grammes. The blood that circulates through the heart chambers does not supply the heart muscle, thus requiring a separate circulatory system for the heart muscle.

parents who were selected based upon their genetic disease profile. Their mothers should have been vaccinated, free of all internal and external parasites and properly nourished. For these reasons, a visit to the veterinary surgeon who cared for the queen is recommended. The queen passes on disease resistance to her kittens, which can last for eight to ten weeks. She can also pass on parasites and many infections. That's why you should visit the veterinary surgeon who cared for the queen.

## VACCINATIONS
Most vaccinations are given by injection and should only be done by a veterinary surgeon. Both he and you should keep a record of the date of the injection, the identification of the vaccine and the amount given. The first vaccination is normally given when the kitten is about 8–9 weeks old. About 30 days later, a booster is given. Although there are many diseases to which a cat may fall victim, the most dangerous three—FIE, FVR and FeLV—can be safeguarded against with a single (three-in-one) injection. Thereafter, an annual booster is all that is required.

## MAJOR DISEASES
There are a number of diseases for which there is either no cure or little chance of recovery. However, some can be prevented by vaccination. All breeders and owners should ensure kittens are so protected.

> ## THE RIB CAGE
> Cats usually have 13 pairs of ribs. The ribs in the middle are longer than the ribs on either end (or beginning) of the rib cage. The first nine ribs are joined to the chest bone (sternum) with costal cartilages. Ribs 10, 11 and 12 are also associated with cartilage, which contributes to the costal arch. The thirteenth rib is called the floating rib and its cartilage is separate from the other ribs.

# BLOOD GROUP INCOMPATIBILITY (BGI)

In recent years, blood group incompatibility has become the focus of scientists, vets and breeders. Its importance to pet owners is when transfusions are needed. For breeders it probably accounts for a large percentage of kittens that die from fading kitten syndrome. Scientifically the problem is called neonatal erythrolysis, meaning the destruction of red blood cells in newly born offspring.

Cats have two blood groups, A & B. Group A is dominant to B (which is genetically called recessive). When the antibodies of B-group mothers are passed to A-group kittens, via her colostrum milk, they destroy red blood cells. Death normally follows within a few days.

Most domestic cats tested are group A. However, national and regional differences display a variation in which 1-6% may be of type B. In pedigreed breeds it has been found that the number of group-B cats varies significantly. The following breeds, based on present available data, have the indicated percentage incidence of group-B blood type.

| | |
|---|---|
| 0% | Siamese, Burmese and Oriental Shorthair |
| 1-5% | Maine Coon, Manx and Norwegian Forest |
| 10-20% | Abyssinian, Birman, Japanese Bobtail, Persian, Scottish Fold and Somali |
| 25-50% | British Shorthair, Devon and Cornish Rex and Exotic Shorthair |

The clear implication to breeders is to establish their cats' blood group, via testing, and conduct appropriate matings. These should not result in B-group mothers nursing A-group kittens.

The safe matings are:

1. Group-A males     x   A  females
2. Group-B males     x   A or B  females
3. Group-A females   x   A or B  males
4. Group-B females   x   B males

Breeders are advised to seek further information before embarking on stock purchase and breeding programmes.

**FELINE INFECTIOUS ENTERITIS (FIE)**
This is also known as feline panleukopenia, feline distemper and feline parvovirus. The virus attacks the intestinal system. It is spread via the faeces and urine. The virus may survive for many years in some environments. The use of household bleach (sodium hypochlorite) for cleaning helps to prevent colonisation. Signs, among others, are diarrhoea, vomiting, depression, anorexia and dehydration. Death may occur within days. A vaccine is available.

**FELINE VIRAL RHINOTRACHEITIS (FVR) & CALCIVIRUS (FCV)**
Also known as cat flu, this is a complex of upper respiratory diseases. Signs are excessive hard sneezing, runny nose and mouth ulcers. Cats vaccinated after having contracted flu may recover but may suffer recurrent bouts, especially if they become stressed.

**CARE OF FELINE KIDNEYS**
The kidney of the cat is larger than that of the dog, but it has the typical bean shape. It receives 25% of the blood output of the heart! For this reason, it has rather significant veins to accommodate this large supply of blood, and injuries suffered by the kidneys are usually serious and not uncommon.

# HEALTH AND VACCINATION SCHEDULE

| AGE | 6 WKS | 8 WKS | 10 WKS | 12 WKS | 16 WKS | 6 MOS | 1 YR |
|---|---|---|---|---|---|---|---|
| Worm control | ✔ | ✔ | ✔ | | ✔ | | |
| Neutering | | | | | | ✔ | |
| Rhinotracheitis | ✔ | ✔ | | ✔ | ✔ | | ✔ |
| Panleukopenia | ✔ | ✔ | | ✔ | | | ✔ |
| Calcivirus | | ✔ | | | ✔ | | ✔ |
| Feline Leukaemia | | | | ✔ | | | ✔ |
| Feline Infectious Peritonitis | | | | ✔ | ✔ | | ✔ |
| Faecal evaluation | | | | | | ✔ | |
| Feline Immunodeficiency testing | | | | | | | ✔ |
| Feline Leukaemia testing | | | | ✔ | | | ✔ |
| Dental evaluation | | ✔ | | | | ✔ | |
| Rabies | | | | ✔ | ✔ | | ✔ |

Vaccinations are not instantly effective. It takes about two weeks for the cat's immune system to develop antibodies. Most vaccinations require annual booster shots. Your veterinary surgeon should guide you in this regard.

# DISEASE REFERENCE CHART

| | What is it? | Cause | Symptoms |
|---|---|---|---|
| **Feline Leukaemia Virus (FeLV)** | Infectious disease; kills more cats each year than any other feline infectious disease. | A virus spread through saliva, tears, urine and faeces of infected cats; bite wounds. | Early on no symptoms may occur, but eventually infected cats experience signs from depression and weight loss to respiratory distress. FeLV also suppresses immune system, making a cat susceptible to almost any severe chronic illness. |
| **Rabies** | Potentially deadly virus that infects warm-blooded mammals. Not seen in the United Kingdom. | A bacterium, often carried by rodents, that enters through mucous membranes and spreads quickly throughout the body. | Aggressiveness, a blank or vacant look in the eyes, increased vocalisation and/or weak or wobbly gait. |
| **Feline Infectious Enteritis (FIE)** *aka Panleukopenia* | Highly contagious virus, potentially deadly. | Ingestion of the virus, which is usually spread through the faeces of infected cats. | Most common: severe diarrhoea. Also vomiting, fatigue, lack of appetite, severe inflammation of intestines. |
| **Feline Viral Rhinotracheitis (FVR)** | Viral disease that affects eyes and upper respiratory tracts. | A virus that can affect any cat, especially those in multiple-cat settings. | Sneezing attacks, coughing, drooling thick saliva, fever, watery eyes, ulcers of mouth, nose and eyes. |
| **Feline Immuno-deficiency Virus (FIV)** | Virus that reduces white blood cells. | An infection spread commonly through cat-fight wounds. | Signs may be dormant for years or innocuous, such as diarrhoea or anaemia. |
| **Feline Infectious Peritonitis (FIP)** | A fatal viral disease, may be linked to FeLV and FIV. | Bacteria in dirty litter boxes; stress may increase susceptibility in kittens. | Extremely variable; range from abdominal swelling to chest problems, eye ailments and body lesions. |
| **Feline Urological Syndrome (FUS)** | A disease that affects the urinary tracts of cats. | Inflammation of bladder and urethra. | Constipation, constant licking of penis or vulva, blood in urine (males), swollen abdomen, crying when lifted. |

## CLEANLINESS IS THE KEY

Crucial to the prevention and spread of disease is the need to maintain meticulous cleanliness, especially relating to the litter tray. Many diseases and problems are transferred via faecal matter. Once a problem is suspected, the advice of a vet should be sought. Blood tests, faecal microscopy and other testing methods are now available. They can mean the difference between life and death for a cherished pet.

## FELINE LEUKAEMIA VIRUS (FELV)

This is a highly infectious viral disease. It is spread via direct contact—mutual grooming, saliva, feeding bowls, faeces, urine and biting. It can be passed prenatally from a female to her offspring. It creates tumours, anaemia, immune system depression, pyrexia (high temperatures), lethargy, respiratory disease, intestinal disease and many other potentially fatal problems. It is most prevalent in high-density cat

## NEUTERING

Neutering is a major means of avoiding ill health. It dramatically reduces the risk of males' becoming involved in territorial battles with the dangers of physical injury and disease transference. It makes the male more placid and less likely to scent mark its home. It also reduces the incidence of prostate problems, and there is no risk of testicular cancer. The female avoids potentially lethal illnesses related to her being allowed to remain in an unmated condition, such as breast cancer.

Neutering is usually performed between four and six months of age, but it can be done as early as eight weeks of age. Data available on the age at which a kitten is neutered indicate that early neutering has more advantages than drawbacks. Breeders should have this performed on all cats sold as pets.

Male cats are neutered. The operation removes the testicles and requires that the cat be anaesthetised. Females are spayed. This is major surgery during which the ovaries and uterus are removed. Both males and females should be kept quiet at home for about seven to ten days following the procedure, at which time the vet will remove the sutures.

populations. Not all cats will be affected, but they may become carriers.

Kittens less than six months old are especially vulnerable. Infected cats usually die by the time they are three to four years old. Cats can be screened or tested for this disease. Vaccination is not 100% effective but is recommended in kittens being sold into multi-cat environments.

### FELINE IMMUNODEFICIENCY VIRUS (FIV)

This causes the white blood cells to be significantly reduced, thus greatly suppressing the efficiency of the immune system. It is not transferable to humans. Infection is normally gained from cat-fight wounds; thus, outdoor males are at the most risk. A cat diagnosed via blood tests as FIV-positive may live a normal life for months or years if retained indoors and given careful attention. Signs may be innocuous in the early stages, such as anaemia or diarrhoea. No vaccine is available.

### FELINE INFECTIOUS PERITONITIS (FIP)

This viral disease is invariably fatal once contracted in its more potent forms. However, the virulence of the virus is variable and may by destroyed by the immune system. Stress may increase susceptibility in kittens. It may be linked to FeLV and FIV. Signs are extremely variable and range from abdominal swelling to chest problems, eye ailments to body lesions. There are various tests available, but none is as yet 100% conclusive. Strict cleanliness is essential, especially of litter trays. No vaccine is available.

## FELINE UROLOGICAL SYNDROME (FUS)

This is a very distressing condition caused by an inflammation of the bladder and urethra. Signs are constipation-like squatting and attempts to urinate, regular licking of the penis or vulva, blood in urine (males), swollen abdomen, crying when lifted and urinating in unusual places (often only small amounts).

The numerous causes include: infection, dirty litter tray of the indoor cat, alkaline urine (in cats it should be acidic), diet too dry, lack of water intake (even though this may be available) and being hit by a vehicle (damaged nerves). Veterinary treatment is essential or the condition could be fatal due to bladder bursting or presence of dangerous bacteria.

## RABIES

Britain and most European Community countries are free of this terrible disease. The stringent quarantine laws of Britain are such that vaccination is not necessary. However, the

## THE PICA SYNDROME

The term 'pica' is a veterinary term that refers to a morbid desire to ingest things that are abnormal to the cat's diet. Cats are often addicted to soft materials like wool, silk, cotton or a mixture of these and synthetic cloths. Hard plastics, wood and even metals have been involved in this pica syndrome. If you observe your cat chewing these fabrics or materials, speak to your vet. Most vets who observe the pica syndrome think it is a nervous problem that can successfully be treated with drugs normally used for depression. In any case, the genetic makeup of your cat should be investigated and if pica occurs in any of the parents or previous offspring, do not breed your cat.

introduction of passports for dogs and cats means that resident British cats must be vaccinated if they are to travel abroad and return to the UK without being placed into quarantine. The vaccination is given when the kitten is three or more months old. The pet passport process takes at least six months to complete, so plan well ahead.

## GINGIVITIS (Plasmocytic-Lymphocytic Stomatitis)

There are many causes of this condition. But the end result is the same—bad breath, excessive plaque, tooth loss and, almost certainly, pain. The cat salivates excessively, starts to eat less and consequently loses weight. On inspection, the gums are swollen, especially in the area of the premolar and molar teeth. They bleed easily. There are various treatments, such as antibiotics, immunostimulants and disinfectant mouth gels. However, these invariably prove short-term and merely delay the inevitable treatment of extraction.

Prevention avoids this painful condition. Regular tooth inspection and cleaning, plus provision of hard-food items, such as cat biscuits, achieve this to a large extent. There are also special cat chews made of dried fish that help clean the teeth. They also contain antibacterial enzymes that minimise or prevent secondary bacteria from accumulating. Ask for these at your pet shop or vet's surgery. Gingivitis may commence in kittens, so do not think it is something that only occurs in older cats.

## COMMON HEALTH PROBLEMS

### DERMATITIS (ECZEMA)

Dry lifeless coat, loss of coat, tiny scabs over the head and body, loose flakes (dandruff) and excessive scratching are all commonly called eczema. The cause covers a range of possibilities including diet, parasitic mites such as *Cheyletiella spp*, fungus or an allergy to flea or other bites. Sometimes reasons are unknown. Veterinary diagnosis and treatment are required.

### RINGWORM (DERMATOPHYTOSIS)

This problem is fungal, not that of a worm. The most common form is *Microsporum canis*, which accounts for over 90% of cases. Cats less than one year old are at the highest risk, while longhaired breeds are more prone to the problem than shorthaired cats. The fungi feed on the keratin layers of the skin, nails and hair. Direct contact and spores that remain in the environment are the main means of transmission.

Typical signs are circular-type bald areas of skin, which may be flaked and reddish. The coat generally may become dry and lifeless, giving the appearance of numerous other skin and hair problems. Veterinary diagnosis and treatment, either topical or via

### HEALTHY CAT

There are more cats than dogs. This has stimulated the veterinary medical community to learn more about cats and to prescribe more modern medicines to keep felines healthier.

# First Aid at a Glance

## BURNS/SCALDS
Place the affected area under cool water; use ice if only a small area is burnt. Do not cover the burn or clip hair away. Petroleum jelly can be applied; take cat to vet immediately.

## CHEMICAL BURNS
Wash with water only. If you know the chemical is acid, a weak solution of sodium bicarbonate will help, or a vinegar solution will do for alkaline burns.

## BEE/INSECT BITES
Apply freshly sliced onion. Apply ice to relieve swelling; antihistamine dosed properly.

## AUTOMOBILE ACCIDENT
Move cat from roadway with blanket; seek veterinary aid.

## ANIMAL BITES
Clean any bleeding area; apply pressure until bleeding subsides; go to the vet.

## SHOCK
Calm the cat, keep him warm and in a horizontal position; seek immediate veterinary aid.

## SPIDER BITES
Use cold compress and a pressurised pack to inhibit venom's spreading.

## NOSEBLEED
Apply cold compress to the nose; apply pressure to any visible abrasion.

## ANTIFREEZE POISONING
Induce vomiting with hydrogen peroxide. Seek *immediate* veterinary help!

## BLEEDING
Apply pressure above the area; treat wound by applying a cotton pack.

## FISH HOOKS
Removal best handled by vet; hook must be cut in order to remove.

## HEAT STROKE
Move animal to cool, shaded area, wet animal with water and place ice packs around head and body; seek immediate veterinary aid.

## SNAKE BITES
Pack ice around bite; contact vet quickly; identify snake for proper antivenin.

## FROSTBITE/HYPOTHERMIA
Warm the cat with a warm bath, electric blankets or hot water bottles.

## ASPHYXIA
Cat must breathe fresh air as soon as possible. Encourage your cat to move around.

## ABRASIONS
Clean the wound and wash out thoroughly with fresh water; apply antiseptic.

*Remember: an injured cat may attempt to bite a helping hand from fear and confusion. Handle your cat in a calm and gentle manner so as to avoid upsetting the animal further.*

drugs, is essential as the condition is zoonotic, meaning it can be transferred to humans.

### EAR PROBLEMS

Most of the common ear problems affect the outer ear. The cat's constant scratching of the ears, holding the ear to one side, greasy hairs around the ear, dark brown wax (cerumen) in the ears, scaly flakes in or around the ear and minute white or orange pinhead-like bodies (mites) in the ear are common signs. Canker is a term used for ear infections, but it has no specific meaning.

Over-the-counter remedies for ear problems are ineffective unless correct diagnosis has been made. It is therefore better to let the vet diagnose and treat the cat. Some problems may require anaesthesia and minor surgery.

### DIARRHOEA

This is a general term used to indicate a semi-liquid to liquid state of faecal matter. Mild to acute cases may be due to a change of home, dietary change, eating an 'off' item, gorging on a favoured food, stress or a minor chill. These often rectify themselves within days. Chronic and persistent diarrhoea may be the result of specific diseases. Any indication of blood in the faecal matter must be considered dangerous.

In minor cases, withholding food for 12–24 hours, or feeding a simple diet, may arrest the condition. If not, wisdom suggests contacting your vet. Faecal analysis and blood testing may be required. By answering numerous questions related to the cat's diet, general health, level of activity, loss of appetite, etc., the vet will determine whether tests are required or if immediate treatment seems more appropriate. Do not give cats human or canine intestinal remedies; these could prove dangerous.

### CONSTIPATION

Constipation—when a cat strains but is unable to pass motions—can have many causes. The cat may have hairballs, may have eaten a bird or rodent and has a bone lodged in its intestinal tract, may be suffering from a urological problem rather than constipation, or may have been hit by a car and has damaged the nerves that control bowel movements. As constipation is potentially serious, veterinary advice should be sought. Laxatives and faecal softener tablets may be given, the faecal matter can be surgically removed or other treatment carried out.

## Recognising a Sick Cat

Unlike colicky babies and cranky children, our feline charges cannot tell us when they are feeling ill. Therefore, there are a number of signs that owners can identify to know that their cats are not feeling well.

**Take note for physical manifestations such as:**

- unusual, bad odour, including bad breath
- excessive moulting
- wax in the ears, chronic ear irritation
- oily, flaky, dull haircoat
- mucous, tearing or similar discharge in the eyes
- fleas or mites
- mucous in stool, diarrhoea
- sensitivity to petting or handling
- licking at paws, scratching face, etc.

**Keep an eye out for behavioural changes as well including:**

- lethargy, idleness
- lack of patience or general irritability
- lack of appetite, digestive problems
- phobias (fear of people, loud noises, etc.)
- strange behaviour, suspicion, fear
- coprophagia
- whimpering, crying

## Get Well Soon

You don't need a DVR or a BVMA to provide good TLC to your sick or recovering cat, but you do need to pay attention to some details that normally wouldn't bother him. The following tips will aid Kitty's recovery and get him back on his paws again:

- Keep his space free of irritating smells, like heavy perfumes and air fresheners.
- Rest is the best medicine! Avoid harsh lighting that will prevent your cat from sleeping. Shade him from bright sunlight during the day and dim the lights in the evening.
- Keep the noise level down. Animals are more sensitive to sound when they are sick.

- Be attentive to any necessary temperature adjustments. A cat with a fever needs a cool room and cold liquids. A queen that is birthing or recovering from surgery will be more comfortable in a warm room, consuming warm liquids and food.
- You wouldn't send a sick child back to school early, so don't rush your cat back into a full routine until he seems absolutely ready.

## EXTERNAL PARASITES

### FLEAS

Of all the problems to which cats are prone, none is more well known and frustrating than fleas. Indeed, flea-related problems are the principal cause of visits to veterinary surgeons. Flea infestation is relatively simple to cure but difficult to prevent. Periodic flea checks for your cat, conducted as well as annual health check-ups, are highly recommended. Consistent dosing with anthelmintic preparations is also advised. Parasites that are harboured inside the body are a bit more difficult to eradicate, but they are easier to control.

To control a flea infestation, you have to understand the flea's life cycle. Fleas are often thought of as a summertime problem but centrally heated homes have changed the life-cycle patterns, and fleas can be found at any time of the year. Fleas thrive in hot and humid environments; they soon die if the temperature drops below 35°F. The most effective method of flea control is a two-stage approach: one stage to kill the adult fleas, and the other to control the development of pre-adult fleas. Unfortunately, no

A male flea.

single active ingredient is effective against all stages of the life cycle.

## LIFE CYCLE STAGES

During its life, a flea will pass through four life stages: egg, larva, pupa and adult. The adult stage is the most visible and irritating stage of the flea life cycle, and this is why the majority of flea-control products concentrate on this stage. The fact is that adult fleas account for only 1% of the total flea population, and the other 99% exist in pre-adult stages, i.e. eggs, larvae and pupae. The pre-adult stages are barely visible to the naked eye.

## THE LIFE CYCLE OF THE FLEA

Eggs are laid on the cat, usually in quantities of about 20 or 30, several times a day. The female adult flea must have a blood meal before each egg-laying session. When first laid, the eggs will not cling to the cat's fur, as the eggs are not sticky. They will immediately fall to the floor or ground, especially if the cat moves around or scratches.

Once the eggs fall from the cat onto the carpet or furniture, they will hatch into yellow larvae, approximately 2 mms long. This takes from 5 to 11 days. Larvae are not particularly mobile and will

## A Look at Fleas

Fleas have been around for millions of years and have adapted to changing host animals. They are able to go through a complete life cycle in less than one month, or they can extend their lives to almost two years by remaining as pupae or cocoons. They must have a blood meal every 10-14 days, and egg production begins within 2 days of their first meal. The female cat flea is very prolific and can lay 2000 eggs in her lifetime!

Fleas have been measured as being able to jump 300,000 times and can jump 150 times their body length in any direction, including straight up. Those are just a few of the reasons why they are so successful in infesting a cat!

S. E. M. BY DR DENNIS KUNKEL, UNIVERSITY OF HAWAII

A scanning electron micrograph (S. E. M.) of a flea.

S. E. M. BY DR DENNIS KUNKEL, UNIVERSITY OF HAWAII

Magnified head of a flea.

usually travel only a few inches from where they hatch. However, they do have a tendency to move away from light and heavy traffic—under furniture, in the carpet and behind doors are common places to find high quantities of flea larvae.

The flea larvae feed on dead organic matter, including adult flea faeces, until they are ready to change into adult fleas. Fleas will usually remain as larvae for around seven days, becoming darker in colour. After this period, the larvae will pupate a protective cocoon. While inside the pupae, the larvae will undergo metamorphosis and change into adult fleas. This can happen within a week, but the adult fleas can remain inside the pupae waiting to hatch for up to six months. The pupae are signalled to hatch by certain stimuli, such as physical pressure—the pupae's being stepped on, heat from an animal lying on the pupae or increased carbon dioxide levels and vibrations—indicating that a suitable host is available.

**DID YOU KNOW?**
Never mix flea-control products without first consulting your veterinary surgeon. Some products can become toxic when combined with others and can cause serious or fatal consequences.

**DID YOU KNOW?**
Flea-killers are poisonous. You should not spray these toxic chemicals on areas of a cat's body that he licks, on his genitals or on his face. Flea killers taken internally are a better answer, but check with your vet in case internal therapy is not advised for your cat.

Once hatched, the adult flea must feed within a few days. Once the adult flea finds a host, it will not leave voluntarily. It only becomes dislodged by grooming or the host animal's scratching. The adult flea will remain on the host for the duration of its life unless forcibly removed.

### TREATING THE ENVIRONMENT AND THE CAT

Treating fleas should be a two-pronged attack. First, the environment needs to be treated; this includes carpets and furniture, especially the cat's bedding and areas underneath furniture. The environment should be treated with a household spray containing an Insect Growth Regulator (IGR) and an insecticide to kill the adult fleas. There are also liquids, given orally, that contain chitin inhibitors. These render flea eggs incapable of development. There are both foam and liquid wipe-on treatments. Additionally, cats can

Opposite page: A scanning electron micrograph of a flea, magnified more than 100x. This image has been colorized for effect.

# The Life Cycle of the Flea

**Eggs**

**Larvae**

**Pupa**

**Adult**

Photos courtesy of Fleabusters' Rx for Fleas

# Flea Control

### IGR (INSECT GROWTH REGULATOR)

Two types of products should be used when treating fleas—a product to treat the pet and a product to treat the home. Adult fleas represent 1% of the flea population. The pre-adult fleas (eggs, larvae and pupae) represent 99% of the flea population and are found in the environment; it is in the case of pre-adult fleas that products containing an Insect Growth Regulator (IGR) should be used in the home.

IGRs are a new class of compounds used to prevent the development of insects. They do not kill the insect outright, but instead use the insect's biology against it to stop it from completing its growth. Products that contain methoprene are the world's first and leading IGRs. Used to control fleas and other insects, this type of IGR will stop flea larvae from developing and protect the house for up to seven months.

### EN GARDE:
### CATCHING FLEAS OFF GUARD!

Consider the following ways to arm yourself against fleas:

• Add a small amount of pennyroyal or eucalyptus oil to your cat's bath. These natural remedies repel fleas.

• Supplement your cat's food with fresh garlic (minced or grated) and a hearty amount of brewer's yeast, both of which ward off fleas.

• Use a flea comb on your cat daily. Submerge fleas in a cup of bleach to kill them quickly.

• Confine the cat to only a few rooms to limit the spread of fleas in the home.

• Vacuum daily...and get all of the crevices! Dispose of the bag every few days until the problem is under control.

• Wash your cat's bedding daily. Cover cushions where your cat sleeps with towels, and wash the towels often.

be injected with treatments that can last up to six months. Emulsions that have the same effect can also be added to food. The advanced treatments are only available from veterinary surgeons. The IGRs actually mimic the fleas' own hormones and stop the eggs and larvae from developing into adult fleas. There are currently no treatments available to attack the pupa stage of the life cycle, so the adult insecticide is used to kill the newly hatched adult fleas before they find a host. Most IGRs are active for many months, while adult insecticides are only active for a few days.

When treating with a household spray, it is a good idea to vacuum before applying the product. This stimulates as many pupae as possible to hatch into adult fleas. The vacuum cleaner should also be treated with a flea treatment to prevent the eggs and larvae that have been hoovered into the vacuum bag from hatching.

The second stage of treatment is to apply an adult insecticide to the cat, usually in the form of a collar or a spray. Alternatively, there are drops that, when placed on the back of the animal's neck, spread throughout the fur and skin to kill adult fleas. A word of warning: Never use products sold for dogs on your cat; the result could be fatal.

PHOTO BY DWIGHT R KUHN

**Dwight R Kuhn's magnificent action photo, showing a flea jumping.**

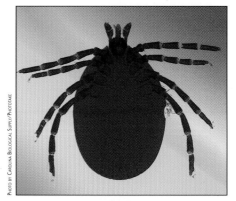

PHOTO BY CAROLINA BIOLOGICAL SUPPLY/PHOTOTAKE

**A brown tick, *Rhipicephalus sanguineus*, is an uncommon but annoying tick found on cats.**

PHOTO BY DR DENNIS KUNKEL, UNIVERSITY OF HAWAII

**The head of a tick, *Dermacentor variabilis*, enlarged and coloured for effect.**

## TICKS AND MITES

Though not as common as fleas, ticks and mites are found all over the tropical and temperate world. They don't bite, like fleas; they harpoon. They dig their sharp proboscis (nose) into the cat's skin and drink the blood. Their only food and drink is your cat's blood. Cats can get potentially fatal anaemia, paralysis and many other diseases from ticks and mites. They may live where fleas are found and they like to hide in cracks or seams in walls wherever cats live. They are controlled the same way fleas are controlled.

The *Dermacentor variabilis* may well be the most common tick in many geographical areas, especially those areas where the climate is hot and humid. The other common ticks that attack small animals are *Rhipicephalus sanguineus, Ixodes* and some species of *Amblyomma*.

Most ticks have life expectancies of a week to six months, depending upon climatic conditions. They can neither jump nor fly, but they can crawl slowly and can range up to 5 metres (16 feet) to reach a sleeping or unsuspecting animal.

### INTERNAL PARASITES

Most animals—fishes, birds and mammals, including cats and humans—have worms and other parasites that live inside their bodies. According to Dr Herbert R Axelrod, the fish pathologist, there are two kinds of parasites: dumb and smart. The smart parasites live in peaceful cooperation with their hosts (symbiosis), while the dumb parasites kill their host. Most of the worm infections are relatively

## TOXOPLASMOSIS AND PREGNANT WOMEN

Toxoplasmosis is caused by a single parasite, *Toxoplasma gondii.* Cats acquire it by eating infected prey, such as rodents or birds, or raw meat. Obviously, strictly indoor cats are at less risk of infection than cats that are permitted to roam outdoors. Symptoms include diarrhoea, listlessness, pneumonia and inflammation of the eye. Sometimes there are no symptoms. The disease can be treated with antibiotics.

The only way humans can get the disease is through direct contact with the cat's faeces. People usually don't display any symptoms, although they can show mild flu-like symptoms. Once exposed, an antibody is produced and the person builds immunity to the disease.

The real danger to humans is that pregnant women can pass the parasite to the developing foetus. In this case the chances are good that the baby will be born with a major health problem and/or serious birth defects. In order to eliminate risk, pregnant women should have someone else deal with the litter-box duties or wear gloves while taking care of the litter box and wash hands thoroughly afterwards.

Opposite page: The tick, *Dermacentor variabilis,* is one of the most common ticks found on cats. Look at the strength in its eight legs! No wonder it's hard to detach them.

# INTERNAL PARASITES OF CATS

| NAME | DESCRIPTION | SYMPTOMS | ACQUISITION | TREATMENT |
|---|---|---|---|---|
| **Roundworm** (*Toxocara cati* and *Toxascaris leonina*) | Large, white, coil-like worms, 2–4 inches long, resembling small springs. | Vomiting, pot belly, respiratory problems, poor growth rate, protruding third eyelids, poor haircoat. | Ingesting infective larvae; ingesting infected mammals, birds or insects; a queen with *Toxocari cati* nursing kittens. | Anthelmintics; scrupulously clean environment (e.g. daily removal of all faeces recommended). |
| ***Physaloptera* species** | 1–6 inches long, attacks the wall of the stomach. | Vomiting, anorexia, melena. | Eating insects that live in soil (e.g. May beetles). | Diagnosed with a gastroscope; treated with pyrantel pamoate. Prevention of exposure to the intermediate hosts. |
| ***Gordius* or Horsehair worm** | 6-inch pale brown worms with stripes. | Vomiting. | May ingest a worm while drinking from or making contact with swimming pools and toilet bowls. | Anthelmintics; avoiding potentially infected environments. |
| **Hookworm** (*Ancylostoma tubaeforme*) | The adult worms, ranging from 6 to 15 mms in length, attach themselves to the small intestines. | Anaemia, melena, weight loss, poor haircoat. | Larva penetrating the cat's skin, usually attacks the small intestine. Found in soil and flower gardens where faecal matter is deposited. | Fortnightly treatment with anthelmintics. Good sanitation (e.g. daily cleanup of litter boxes). |
| **Tapeworm** (*Dipylidium caninum* and *Taenia taeniformis*) | Up to 3 feet long. Parts shaped similar to cucumber seeds. The most common intermediate hosts are fleas and biting lice. | No clinical signs—difficult to detect. | Eating infected adult fleas. Uses rodents as hosts. | Praziquantel and epsirantel. Management of environment to ensure scrupulously clean conditions. Proper flea control. |

easy to control. If they are not controlled, they weaken the host cat to the point that other medical problems occur, but they are not dumb parasites.

### HOOKWORMS

The worm *Ancylostoma tubaeforme* can inject a cat by larva penetrating its skin. It attaches itself to the small intestine of the cat, where it sucks blood. This loss of blood could cause iron-deficiency anaemia.

Outdoor cats that spend much of their time in the garden or in contact with soil are commonly injected with hookworm. There is another worm, the *Gordius* or a horsehair worm, that, if ingested by a cat, causes vomiting.

### TAPEWORMS

There are many species of tapeworms. They are carried by

### DEWORMING

Ridding your kitten of worms is VERY IMPORTANT because certain worms that kittens carry, such as tapeworms and roundworms, can infect humans.

Breeders initiate a deworming programme at or about four weeks of age. The routine is repeated every two or three weeks until the kitten is three months old. The breeder from whom you obtained your kitten should provide you with the complete details of the deworming programme.

Your veterinary surgeon can prescribe and monitor the programme of deworming for you. The usual programme is treating the kitten every 15–20 days until the kitten is positively worm-free.

It is advised that you only treat your kitten with drugs that are recommended professionally.

The head and rostellum (the round prominence on the scolex) of a tapeworm, which infects cats and humans.

fleas! The cat eats the flea and starts the tapeworm cycle. Humans can also be infected with tapeworms, so don't eat fleas! Fleas are so small that your cat could pass them onto your hands, your plate or your food and thus make it possible for you to ingest a flea that is carrying tapeworm eggs.

While tapeworm infection is not life-threatening in cats (smart parasite!), it can be the cause of a

Magnified heartworm larvae, *Dirofilaria immitis.*

Photo by Carolina Biological Supply/Phototake

The heartworm, *Dirofilaria immitis.*

Photo by James E Hayden, RPB/Phototake

very serious liver disease for humans. About 50 percent of the humans infected with *Echinococcus multilocularis*, a type of tapeworm that causes alveolar hydatis, perish.

### HEARTWORMS
Heartworms are thin, extended worms up to 30 cms (12 ins) long, which are difficult to diagnose in cats as the worms are too few to be identified by the antigen-detection test. Symptoms may be loss of energy, loss of appetite, coughing, the development of a pot belly and anaemia. Heartworm infection in cats should be treated very seriously as it is often fatal.

Heartworms are transmitted by mosquitoes. The mosquito drinks the blood of an infected cat and takes in larvae with the blood. It takes two to three weeks for the larvae to develop to the infective stage within the body of the mosquito. Cats are less frequently infected with heartworms than dogs are. Also, the parasite is more likely to attack the cat's brain or other organs rather than the heart. Cats should be treated at about six weeks of age, and maintained on a prophylactic dose given monthly.

## THE FELINE EYE

*by Lorraine Waters BvetNed, CertVOphthal, MRCVS*

This part of the book aims to provide an owner's guide to feline ophthalmology. Ophthalmology is the study of eyes.

Eye diseases in the cat usually result from trauma, infection or neoplasia. Unlike the dog, the cat has few inherited eye conditions. Most of the conditions to be discussed are not amenable to first-aid measures or home remedies. Therefore, if you are at all worried about your cat's eyes, you should seek prompt veterinary attention.

Ocular pain is frequently associated with eye disease and can be recognised in your cat because it will show a combination of the following signs: blinking, increased tear production, fear of light and rubbing at the eye. Some conditions result in loss of vision; a gradual loss of vision may go unnoticed, as the cat slowly adapts, but a sudden loss produces an obvious change in behaviour. Being blind may not be as bad as it sounds, as cats adapt and cope amazingly well in familiar surroundings.

To examine the eye properly, veterinary surgeons first use a bright light, which allows close examination of the lids, conjunctiva, cornea and iris. Following this, an ophthalmoscope can be used, in a darkened room, to give a magnified view. Then by using the lenses within the ophthalmoscope, it is possible to focus on the structures further back in the eye, such as the lens, vitreous and retina.

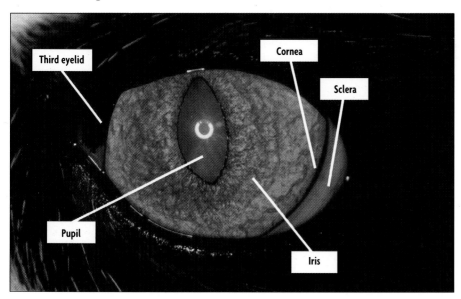

Third eyelid

Cornea

Sclera

Pupil

Iris

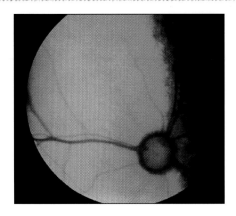

The feline fundus, the eye as seen through the veterinary surgeon's ophthalmoscope.

Topical ointments and drops are often prescribed for the treatment of eye disease. There are a few simple rules to follow when administering them. It is important to clean away discharges before applying treatment. Only give one drop or just a few millimetres of ointment; if you give too much, it will be diluted by increased tear production. Systemic drugs are those given by mouth to achieve higher concentrations at the back of the eye or for diseases which involve other body systems.

## DISEASES OF THE FELINE EYE

### GLOBE AND ORBIT

The eye sits in a bony socket in the skull known as the orbit. In short-nosed breeds, the orbit is shallow and the normal-sized eyes bulge forward. This situation can predispose the eye to a number of problems, such as exposure keratitis, overflow of tears and even prolapse of the globe (eye). Cats can be born with eyes that are too small and sink back into the orbit, to be covered by the third eyelid. This is non-inherited and usually associated with damage to the eye in utero. Abnormal enlargement of the globe may be congenital (buphthalmos) or acquired (hydrophthalmos) and is the end point of glaucoma.

The globe can prolapse from the orbit following head trauma, a common injury for cats involved in road traffic accidents. A minor prolapse replaced early can result in restoration of normal function. However, there is often stretching of the optic nerve and tearing of the extra-ocular muscles. In these cases the eye may be permanently damaged and have to be surgically removed. As an emergency measure, applying a moist cloth to the prolapsed eye on the way to the surgery will help preserve it.

Problems behind the eye become evident when they cause the eye to bulge forward along with the third eyelid. These include tooth root abscesses, foreign bodies, tumours and occasionally haemorrhage.

### EYELIDS

The eyes of a kitten should open around 10–14 days of age. Once this has occurred, it is possible to see if the lids have been properly formed. Failure of all or part of the eyelids to develop is a rare congenital problem, known as coloboma. The unprotected cornea, in the affected area, may become damaged and the lid must be surgically restored. Early infection in the eye may delay or prevent eyelid opening; the lids can be opened surgically to allow bathing and appropriate medication to be given.

Entropion and ectropion are common conditions in the dog and are related to conformation. Fortunately these are rare in cats and can be surgically corrected. Entropion secondary to ocular pain may remain once the cause of the pain is removed. Fortunately, these cases will respond to corrective surgery. Extra or abnormally positioned hairs are frequently seen as an inherited problem in dogs, but are rare in cats.

There are several types of tumours that can occur on the eyelids. The most common type is squamous cell carcinoma, more prevalent in white and part-white cats, as ultra-violet light (sunlight) plays a role in causing this condition. Treatment may consist of cryotherapy, surgical excision or radiation treatment. Early

recognition and treatment is essential to prevent destructive local spreading.

## CONJUNCTIVA

The pink tissue lining the eyelid and covering the third eyelid and front of the sclera is called the conjunctiva. Dermoids are elements of skin tissue that arise in abnormal places. Dermoids often, but not invariably, contain hairs and can form on the conjunctiva and/or cornea. Dermoids act as foreign bodies in the eye, causing irritation and pain, and need to be surgically removed.

The most frequently encountered problem with the conjunctiva is conjunctivitis. In cats the majority of cases are infectious. An eye with conjunctivitis usually looks red and swollen with signs of ocular pain. Discharges may be watery or sticky yellow, indicating bacterial infection.

The most common infectious cause of feline conjunctivitis is feline herpesvirus (FHV). Feline calicivirus (FCV) can also cause conjunctivitis and is usually

*Eyelid coloboma is a rare congenital problem in cats.*

*Dermoid in a longhaired cat.*

Conjunctivitis, frequently an infectious disease in cats.

Corneal ulcer stained with fluorescein.

associated with other signs, such as upper respiratory tract signs and mouth ulcers. The bacteria *Chlamydia psittaci* can cause conjunctivitis in individual cats and in multi-cat households. Individual cases respond well to appropriate antibiotic therapy. Chronic and recurrent conjunctivitis in multi-cat situations requires thorough and prolonged treatment, management changes and, where appropriate, vaccination. *Mycoplasma spp.* can cause a less severe conjunctivitis than *Chlamydia spp.* Opportunistic infection can occur following cat-fight wounds, as bacteria are found on cats' teeth and claws.

Non-infectious causes of conjunctivitis include trauma,

Tear staining is more commonly seen in short-nosed cat breeds.

foreign bodies, allergic disease, tumours and pre-corneal tear film abnormalities. Eosinophilic keratoconjunctivitis is a disease where the conjunctiva and cornea are invaded by cells from the immune system, primarily mast cells and eosinophils. These cells are responsible for inflammation and allergic reactions. This tends to occur in young to middle-aged cats and may be seasonal. Treatment usually works well but may be required long-term.

Several forms of neoplasia (cancer) can affect the conjunctiva in cats and can be either primary tumours arising in the conjunctiva or secondary, spreading from elsewhere in the body.

### SCLERA
The sclera is the white fibrous coat of the globe. It is partially covered by the conjunctiva and protects the more fragile internal structures. Congenital defects of this structure are very rare. Inflammation (scleritis and episcleritis) is a problem in dogs and humans but extremely rare in cats. Feline

scleral diseases are usually associated with trauma and neoplasia.

### PRE-CORNEAL TEAR FILM

This forms from tears and moistens, lubricates and helps protect the cornea. Decreased tear production occurs if the tear glands are not working properly and results in a condition called 'dry eye' or keratoconjunctivis sicca (KCS). The cornea becomes dry and roughened, leading to keratitis and ulceration. It can occur following FHV infection, trauma, facial paralysis and chronic inflammation.

Overproduction of tears can be seen as a result of ocular pain. The naso-lacrimal duct drains the tears; it runs from the inner corner of the eye to just inside the end of the nose. Congenital defects, such as a small duct opening, result in tear overflow and staining around the eye. These can usually be corrected surgically. Acquired blockages may result from chronic conjunctivitis or foreign bodies.

Tear staining is also seen in short-nosed breeds because the duct is tortuous and drainage inadequate. This is also associated with medial lower lid entropion, occluding the duct opening. This anatomical combination is very difficult to improve surgically.

**Corneal foreign body.**

### CORNEA

The cornea is the clear circular area at the front of the eye through which the iris and pupil can be seen. Light passes through and is focused by the cornea, before passing through the lens and hence onto the retina. Congenital defects are rare but include micro- and megalocornea. There is sometimes a transient cloudiness following opening of the eyes but it should disappear by four weeks of age.

One of the most common problems involving the cornea is ulceration, where the top layer of corneal cells (the epithelium) is lost and the nerve endings exposed, resulting in ocular pain. Fluorescein is a special stain that can be used to demonstrate ulcers; they show up as a yellow/green

**Corneal sequestrum.**

**Symblepharon, adhesion of the eyelid to the eyeball.**

patch on the cornea. If your cat has had this performed, you may have noticed the stain appearing at the end of its nose; this is because it drains down the naso-lacrimal duct and demonstrates that it is not blocked.

The most common cause of ulceration is trauma, from fight wounds or foreign bodies. FHV can cause ulceration. There is also a form of ulceration where the epithelium does not stick down again after healing and can easily become detached. This is seen as a breed-related problem in dogs. In cats it can be seen in older animals or associated with FHV infection, resulting in recurrent ulcer formation.

The cornea is very quick to repair ulcers, and, provided that the initial cause is removed, healing should only take a few days. Antibiotics are often applied to the eye while ulcers heal to prevent bacterial infection. Ulcers need prompt veterinary attention as they can deteriorate rapidly;

deep ulcers can lead to rupture of the eye and require urgent surgical repair.

The cornea is a common site for cat-scratch injuries and some may even penetrate the full thickness into the anterior chamber. If these wounds are repaired quickly and appropriate medical therapy is used, vision can usually be preserved. More severe ones may require reconstructive surgery, removal of the lens or even surgical removal of the eye.

Corneal foreign bodies usually result in ocular pain and need to be removed. Non-painful ones also need to be removed as they may penetrate the eye, causing internal problems.

Corneal sequestrum or necrosis is a condition specific to cats. The corneal stroma (middle layer) degenerates, turns brown/black and emerges through the epithelium, causing ulceration and a foreign body reaction with signs of ocular pain. These lesions usually need to be removed surgically because of the discomfort they cause, but a few will slough off naturally. Often a sequestrum will recur in the same eye or occur in the opposite eye at a later date. This condition is most commonly seen in Colourpoint Persians and is thought to have an inherited component. It may be related to their prominent eye position. The next most common breed with sequestra is the Burmese.

Following healing of a corneal wound, there is usually formation of a scar, which shows up as a white mark, but unless they are extensive they do not usually affect vision.

### TREATMENT AND MANAGEMENT OF FHV-RELATED EYE DISEASES

A combination of treatments is often required to treat feline herpesvirus (FHV) infection. In acute cases kittens are often very sick and need supportive treatment and intensive nursing. Systemic and topical antibiotics are used, sometimes in combination with topical antiviral drugs. Cats that develop symblepharon after acute infection may be blinded by the condition and require new reconstructive surgical techniques. The chronic cases can be difficult to diagnose and challenging to treat. Topical antivirals can be used and in non-ulcerated cases combined with corticosteroids. More recent treatments include L-lysine (to inhibit viral replication), Cimetidine and α-interferon (to boost the local immune response).

The reason for chronic FHV disease is that individuals become carriers of the virus. When they are stressed, the virus is reactivated and signs of infection and the cat's immune response to it manifest in the eye. This can be a major problem in multi-cat households with carrier animals infecting kittens and adults alike. In these cases management changes, including the identification of carriers, use of early vaccinations and isolation of new arrivals, must be instituted.

### AQUEOUS HUMOUR

The aqueous humour is a watery fluid that is responsible for maintaining pressure within the eye. If the drainage angle is blocked and aqueous cannot drain away, pressure within the eye builds up, causing glaucoma. Glaucoma due to a congenitally obstructed drainage system is an inherited problem in many breeds of dog but is rare in the cat. When glaucoma does occur in cats, it is usually acquired, with drainage blocked by inflammatory or neoplastic cells.

Anterior uveitis can result in white blood cells in the anterior chamber, which gives it a cloudy look known as aqueous flare. Infection following penetrating wounds can result in pus accumulating in the chamber, known as hypopyon. Trauma to the eye and intra-ocular tumours may lead to bleeding into the anterior

Herpesvirus ulcer.

Iris pigment
change in an
old cat.

chamber (space behind the cornea and in front of the iris), known as hyphaema. This blood usually forms a clot and is absorbed. Foreign bodies can also occasionally be seen in the anterior chamber.

### IRIS AND CILIARY BODY

The iris and ciliary body are muscular and vascular structures, which lie behind the cornea and in front of the lens. The iris is pigmented and gives the cat's eye its colour. Congenital defects are rare but occasionally cats are born with pieces of the iris missing. Changes in iris colour can occur for a number of reasons; as young cats mature their iris colour may deepen. Inflammation results in reddening of the iris, due to an increase in blood vessel formation and engorgement, and is known as rubeosis iridis. Following inflammation, the iris can remain permanently dark.

As cats age, they can develop a condition called melanosis. This is usually, but not always, a diffuse change, occurring slowly in both eyes. It must be monitored and differentiated from iris melanoma. Melanoma is a tumour of the pigment cells that can result in either diffuse or nodular discoloration of the iris. It usually progresses quickly and only in one eye. This type of neoplasia has the potential to spread outside the eye and is usually treated by surgically removing the affected eye.

A difference in colour between the two irises is known as heterochromia iridis and can occur naturally in white or poorly pigmented breeds, usually associated with congenital deafness. In other cats, it usually indicates a problem in one eye or the other.

The ciliary body and iris are known as the anterior uvea, while the choroid (the vascular layer that lies between the retina and the sclera and provides a blood supply to the retina) is the posterior uvea. Uveitis is an inflammation of the

Iris melanoma, exhibited as a tumour of pigment cells that results in discoloration of the iris.

uvea. It may involve both the anterior and posterior uvea and has many causes in the cat. The main infectious causes are feline immunodeficiency virus (FIV), feline leukaemia virus (FeLV), feline infectious peritonitis (FIP) and toxoplasmosis. Tuberculosis has been reported in cats as a cause of uveitis and, in sub-tropical and tropical countries, fungal infection can be a significant cause. The signs of uveitis for all these diseases are very similar and may include a constricted pupil, rubeosis iridis, aqueous flare, poor vision and ocular pain. It can be difficult to determine the cause in some cases despite thorough investigation. Even if the primary viral infection cannot be cured, cats with uveitis can be treated symptomatically to ease discomfort and maintain vision. Long-term uveitis can lead to cataract formation, lens luxation and glaucoma. Non-infectious causes of uveitis include trauma and neoplasia.

Atrophy of the iris may occur as a result of ageing or following

inflammation. Cysts of the iris are sometimes seen and look like black balloons. They form on the back of the iris but can detach and float through the pupil to rest in front. They are not neoplastic and do not usually need to be removed.

### Lens

The lens is the clear disc-shaped structure suspended behind the iris, responsible for focusing light onto the retina. A cataract, or opacity of the lens and/or its capsule, is a disorder of the lens. Many forms of hereditary cataract are seen in dogs but not in cats. Congenital cataracts are occasionally found as a non-inherited problem. Most of the cataracts seen in cats are formed secondary to lens damage, e.g. blunt trauma, penetrating wounds, chronic anterior uveitis and lens luxation. If cataracts involve the whole lens, light will not be able to get through to the retina and the eye will be rendered blind. If appropriate, cataracts can be surgically removed.

If the lens's suspensory fibres weaken or break, it will become dislocated and can fall either into

Uveitis, inflammation of the iris, ciliary body and choroid.

Cataract developed from long-term uveitis.

the back or front of the eye. This is a common breed-related problem in terrier dogs and is occasionally seen in cats, usually as a result of trauma, ageing or cataract. The lens is usually surgically removed to prevent it from blocking the pupil, which can lead to glaucoma.

The lens condenses with age, giving it a grey appearance, known as senile sclerosis. This is not a true cataract as light can still pass through to the back of the eye and vision is not impaired.

One rare but important condition of the lens in the cat is post-traumatic sarcoma. If the lens is damaged by trauma, it can become neoplastic and rapidly fill the eye with tumours. Appropriate treatment at the time of the initial injury should prevent this, but when it does occur, surgical removal of the eye is recommended.

### VITREOUS HUMOUR

The vitreous humour is a jelly-like substance that fills the space between the back of the lens and the front of the retina. Like the aqueous humour, the vitreous can be infiltrated with haemorrhage and inflammatory cells. Foreign bodies can occasionally be found in the vitreous. Inflammation of the vitreous, known as hyalitis, can be seen as part of generalised uveitis.

Vitreous degenerates with age, giving a cloudy appearance to the back of the eye, but this does not usually affect vision to any great extent.

---

## THINGS TO LOOK OUT FOR

A change in appearance of the eye
- Redness
- Cloudiness
- Change in iris colour

Increase in discharges
- Watery

Sticky mucoid
- Yellow
- Bloody

Blinking, squinting and head shyness
Aversion to light
Rubbing at the eye
Loss of vision
Protrusion of the eye
Loss of facial symmetry

---

### RETINA

The retina, at the back of the eye, is where the visual image is formed. Congenital retinal problems are rare in cats, but colobomas (defects or holes) can occasionally be seen in the optic disc (the point at which nerves converge to leave the eye as the optic nerve). Inflammation of the retina usually occurs together with inflammation of the choroid and is called chorioretinitis or posterior uveitis. The causes are the same as those for anterior uveitis. Inflammation can lead to retinal detachment, haemorrhage, degeneration and scarring of the retina. It can be difficult to diagnose the cause of posterior uveitis; symptomatic treatment is generally given to maintain vision.

The retina may also degenerate

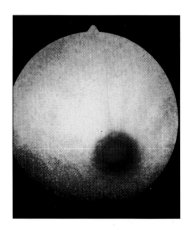

as a result of non-inflammatory processes. An inherited form of retinal degeneration has been described in the Abyssinian and Siamese breeds. Deficiency in dietary taurine (an amino acid) causes retinal degeneration. Fortunately, this is now rare as proprietary cat foods are supplemented with this compound. It may, however, still be a problem with some home prepared diets.

Hypertension is a common cause of retinal disease in elderly cats. It may be primary, essential hypertension or secondary to other diseases, such as kidney disease, hyperthyroidism and diabetes. Hypertension causes changes in the retinal arteries, retinal and vitreal haemorrhages, retinal detachment and hyphaema. Early recognition and treatment are essential to prevent permanent ocular damage and damage to other organs, such as the kidney, heart and brain.

Retinal detachment causes blindness and may result from hypertension, inflammation and neoplasia. If the retina does not reattach in 24–48 hours, there will be permanent vision loss. Symptomatic treatment is often given to reattach the retina, but it is also important to treat the underlying cause.

Retinal haemorrhages can occur as a result of hypertension, inflammation and trauma. They can cause temporary loss of vision but will often be resorbed. Once again it is important to find the underlying cause and treat it accordingly without delay.

Finally, if in any doubt regarding the condition of your cat's eyes, it is always worthwhile consulting your veterinary surgeon. Even if you consider the condition minor, it may not remain so!

**Advanced retinal degeneration.**

**Retinal haemorrhages as a result of hypertension.**

The author is grateful to the Animal Health Trust (England) for the illustrations used in the eye health section.

# USEFUL ADDRESSES

**GREAT BRITAIN**
**The Governing Council of the Cat Fancy (GCCF)**
4-6 Penel Orlieu, Bridgewater, Somerset, TA6 3PG
Email: GCCF_CATS@compuserve.com   Fax: 01278 446627 Tel: 01278 427575

**The Cat Association of Britain**
Mill House, Letcombe Regis, Oxon OX12 9JD      Tel: 01235-766-543

**EUROPE**
**Federation Internationale Feline (FIFe)**
Gen. Sec: Ms Penelope Bydlinski.
Little Dene, Lenham Heath, Maidstone, Kent ME17 2BS, GB
Email: penbyd@compuserve.com   Fax: 1622 850193 Tel: 1622 850908

**World Cat Federation**
Hubertsrabe 280, D-45307, Essen, Germany
Email: wcf@nrw-online.de      Fax: 201-552747 Tel: 201-555724

**AUSTRALIA**
**The Australian Cat Federation, Inc.**
PO Box 3305, Port Adelaide, SA 5015
Email: acf@catlover.com   Fax: 08 8242 2767 Tel: 08 8449 5880

**CANADA**
**Canadian Cat Association**
220 Advance Boulevard, Suite 101, Brampton, Ontario L6T 4J5
Email: office@cca-afc.com   Fax: 99050 459-4023 Tel: 99060459-1481

**SOUTH AFRICA**
**Cat Federation of Southern Africa**
PO Box 25, Bromhof 2154, Gauteng Province, Republic of South Africa

**USA**
**American Cat Association**
8101 Katherine Avenue, Panorama City, CA 91402
Fax: (818) 781-5340 Tel: (818) 781-5656

**American Cat Fanciers Association**
PO Box 203, Point Lookout, MO 65726
Email: info@acfacat.com   Fax: (417) 334-5540 Tel: (417) 334-5430

**Cat Fanciers Association, Inc.**
PO Box 1005, Manasquan, NJ 08736-0805
Email: cfa@cfainc.org    Fax: (732) 528-7391 Tel: (732) 528-9797

**Cat Fanciers Federation**
PO Box 661, Gratis, OH 45330
Email: Lalbert933@aol.com Fax: (937) 787-4290 Tel: (937) 787-9009

**The International Cat Association (TICA)**
PO Box 2684, Harlingen, TX 78551
Email: ticaeo@xanadu2.net Tel: (956) 428-8046